APR 17 1979

A

# PRIVATEERS OF SEVENTY-SIX

# Privateers of Seventy-Six

★★★★★★★

## by FRED J. COOK

*illustrated by*
*William L. Verrill, Jr.*

The Bobbs-Merrill Company, Inc.

INDIANAPOLIS / NEW YORK

LIBRARY OF CONGRESS CATALOGING IN PUBLICATION DATA

Cook, Fred J
    Privateers of seventy-six.

    1. Privateering—Juvenile literature.   2. United
States—History—Revolution, 1775–1783—Naval operations—
Juvenile literature.   I. Title.
E271.C78        973.3′5        75-30808
ISBN 0-672-52127-X

★★★★★★★

# Contents

# Contents

# PRIVATEERS OF SEVENTY-SIX

# I

★★★★★★★

# Washington's Fleet

GEORGE WASHINGTON was wrestling with a problem that would have daunted any general. In this summer of 1775, he commanded the ragtag army of farmers and small townsmen who had chased the British from Lexington and Concord, had mowed them down in rows at Bunker Hill, and now had them surrounded in Boston. Washington's trouble was that his was an army in name only; great numbers of his soldiers lacked guns, and those who had them lacked ammunition.

The powder that the patriots had hoarded before the outbreak of the Revolution had been expended at Bunker Hill, where their deadly fire had winnowed the ranks of the flower of the British Army. By the time Washington arrived in Cambridge to take command, the patriots' munitions had been virtually exhausted. An inventory showed that, except for scanty supplies in the men's powder horns, there was a reserve of only nine rounds per man—and none for the artillery. Receiving this

1

report, Washington was appalled, "so struck that he did not utter a word for a half-hour."

The situation was so desperate that pickets guarding the roads around Boston carried pikes and spears instead of guns, and Benjamin Franklin seriously suggested that the army be supplied with bows and arrows. What choice was there? The rebelling colonies had virtually no native industries—no factories capable of turning out the thousands of muskets that were needed, no means of supplying sufficient powder for small arms and artillery.

The British Army garrisoned in Boston, like other hostile forces in other cities throughout the course of the Revolution, had no such problems. It was bountifully supplied. Day after day, frustrated patriots saw the sails of incoming troop and supply ships popping up over the horizon and making for port with reinforcements, arms and munitions of all kinds. The parade of incoming vessels seemed almost endless, and Washington began to consider the possibility of intercepting some of them. Such an attempt, if successful, would deprive the British of needed supplies and, at the same time, divert into the patriots' hands the guns and ammunition that were so desperately needed. The result of such thinking was the creation of a small fleet of raiders—George Washington's privateers.

As the name implies, privateers were privately owned vessels converted into warships for the purpose of taking prizes and making their owners and crews wealthy. They fell into two classes: vessels that were issued letters of marque, primarily cargo carriers but armed sufficiently to take any weaker enemy craft that might blunder in their way; and outright privateers, carrying large crews and fitted out for just one purpose —commerce raiding and the taking of prizes.

During the Revolution, privateers were licensed by a wide variety of governmental agencies. The Continental Congress issued the most important licenses, but each of the various states, in addition to creating its own state navy, franchised a swarm of privateers on its own. In addition, wily Benjamin Franklin in Paris, doing his best to embroil France in America's war, licensed a number of privateers to raid in British waters.

Washington actually had no authority to send out privateers that became a kind of quasi-navy; but the exigency was acute, and he decided that, as commander-in-chief of the army, it was only logical for him to take any step needed for the preservation of the army. And so he turned to Colonel John Glover, who commanded a Marblehead regiment composed of sailors and fishermen, and delegated to Glover the task of converting some small fishing schooners into commerce raiders.

Work began on the first of these pipsqueak warships, the schooner *Hannah*, in early August, 1775. Gunports were cut in her sides, some small cannon mounted, and her timbers strengthened to support the weight of this new armament. Little is known about the dimensions of the *Hannah*; but she was apparently, like others in the little fleet that Washington commissioned, a tiny craft falling somewhere in the lower 40-to-70-ton range. She was manned by Glover's Marbleheaders, who were to achieve fame later as "the web-footed infantry" that ferried Washington's beaten army from Long Island. Less glorious were the first forays of the web-footers in the *Hannah*. A poor warship, she captured no important prizes and was soon chased ashore on a bar just inside Beverly harbor by a pursuing British warship.

Undeterred, Washington armed and manned other small raiders. One was a seventy-four-ton schooner named the *Lee*. She carried a popgun armament of four four-pounder cannon (meaning the guns fired a round iron ball weighing that amount) and two tiny two-pounders. Her commander was John Manley, a forty-two-year-old Boston shipmaster who in his youth had served some time in the Royal Navy. Manley took the *Lee* to sea in early November, 1775—and soon made history.

Washington's spies in Boston had learned that the British were greatly concerned for the safety of a missing ordnance transport, the brig *Nancy*. The unarmed vessel had become separated from her convoy during a stormy North Atlantic crossing, and several British frigates had been sent out to search the sea lanes and bring her into port.

The frigates failed, but Manley, who was also searching for the *Nancy*, was luckier. Near dusk on November 27, a lookout aboard the *Lee* sighted the topsails of a large brig coming up over the horizon. She was flying British colors and plowing through the seas on a course for Boston. Manley promptly cracked on canvas and brought the *Lee* boiling up alongside the *Nancy*. The British captain, evidently mistaking the puny *Lee* for a pilot boat sent out to guide his vessel into port, brought the *Nancy* up into the wind, her sails aback, and waited to be boarded. Manley was happy to oblige.

A boarding party of eight men, their arms concealed, dropped down into a boat lowered by the *Lee* and rowed across to the brig. The British captain, worn out by battling three weeks of continual gales and storms, was impatient to welcome them. His relief gave way to instant shock as the boat crew swarmed aboard; for, says a British account, "No sooner had they got aboard than they drew their hangers and pistols." The surprise was complete; the brig carried without a blow being struck.

Manley escorted the *Nancy* into Gloucester, and there discovered that he had captured a veritable seagoing arsenal. True, the *Nancy* carried little powder, but she was loaded with almost everything else that Washington so badly needed: 2,000 muskets, 31 tons of musket shot, 30,000 round shot of various sizes, 100,000 musket flints, 11 mortar beds and a huge 13-inch mortar that promised to be of inestimable value in the siege of Boston. The cargo was valued at 10,500 British pounds sterling, a veritable fortune in the money values of those days, but its worth to Washington was beyond price.

The general had just written to Congress, stressing the plight of his army. His men needed muskets—and now he had them; they lacked flints for their guns—and now they had them. The good news was delivered to Washington while he was having tea at headquarters. A messenger rushed in with word of the *Nancy*'s capture and a copy of her manifest; and Mrs. John Morgan, wife of the new director general of hospitals, later wrote: "What delighted me excessively was seeing the pleasure which shown on every countenance, particularly General (Horatio) Gate's; he was in ecstasy. And as General Washington was reading the invoice there was scarce an article that he did not comment upon, and that with so much warmth as diverted everyone present."

The capture of the *Nancy* was as great a shock to

the British as it was a boon to Washington. Sir William Howe, who commanded the British troops in Boston, wrote that the Yankees "are now furnished with all the Requisites for setting the Town on Fire, having got a large Quantity of round Carcasses and other stores, with which they could not have been otherwise Supplied."

While Washington was still exulting over the windfall from the *Nancy*, Manley put to sea again and within a few days captured another important prize, the 300-ton ship *Concord*. Before the end of the year, he took three other British vessels, one bearing important dispatches from Lord Dunmore, the Royal governor of Virginia.

When 1776 dawned, Washington's fleet had increased to six small warships; and Manley, as the outstanding captain, was named commodore and given command of the *Hancock*. Energetic and enterprising, Manley was the first of the captains to get to sea, and he sailed daringly almost to the entrance of Boston harbor, with the tall masts of the anchored British fleet in plain sight. Here, on January 25, almost under the very noses of the British sea dogs, he snapped up two incoming supply ships and started to convoy them to Plymouth. The *General Gage*, an eight-gun British schooner, set out in pursuit; and a broadside-to-broadside duel followed as Manley battled his heavier antagonist to give his prizes a chance to escape.

Both ships were badly cut up, but Manley achieved his purpose. His prizes got safely away, and he battered the *General Gage* so badly that she turned and fled to sanctuary under the guns of the heavier British warships inside the harbor. It was well she did, for Manley had only six more rounds of powder left for his guns when his foe broke off the action.

Others in Washington's little fleet now began to score against the British, especially after the American army, with guns mounted on the heights overlooking Boston, forced Howe to leave. The evacuation, begun in March, was a slow process; and since there had been no way to communicate with England, British troop and supply ships continued to straggle in from the sea long after the bulk of the British forces had departed.

A squadron of British warships lingered in Nantasket Roads in the outer harbor to protect these late arrivals, but the disruption of British plans provided Washington's privateersmen with a unique opportunity. The man who took full advantage of it was James Mugford, in command of the *Franklin*.

Mugford was cruising just off the harbor entrance on May 17 when he spied a large ship lumbering in his direction. The *Franklin* closed with the stranger quickly, and Mugford sent a boarding party to take possession of her. The prize was the ship *Hope*, and a quick look at her manifest showed that she was worth even more than Manley's *Nancy*. For the *Hope* was loaded with 1,500 barrels of powder and other munitions, valued at between 40,000 and 50,000 pounds.

This rich prize presented Mugford with an immediate and crucial problem. How was he to get her safely into port? Since the *Hope* had been taken in full view of the British fleet, Mugford did not dare head for a distant harbor. Pursuit, he knew, would be under way at once, and there was no possibility that the slow, heavily laden *Hope* could escape or that the tiny *Franklin* could fight off the Royal warships to protect her. There was, Mugford decided, only one solution—and this involved a desperate gamble. Ordering all sail made, he headed directly into Boston as if he meant to run into the heart of the British fleet. Then, while the British were still making sail in a wild flurry of activity, he changed course and popped through a narrow channel called Pulling Point Gut that led into the inner harbor. The channel was so shallow and treacherous that British warships dared not follow; and Mugford got safely away with the *Hope*, whose cargo the patriots began to unload right before British eyes.

This was tweaking the Royal Navy's nose with a vengeance, and the British determined to capture the *Franklin* if they could. Two days later they got their chance when the Pulling Point Gut channel proved too tricky even for Mugford. Accompanied by a small privateer, the *Lady Washington*, Mugford was attempting to take the *Franklin* through the narrow passage and out to sea when his little privateer ran hard and fast aground on a sand bar. Efforts to float her were futile, and Mugford knew that the British, seeing his plight, would send out a boarding party to try to carry his vessel under cover of night.

The *Lady Washington*, skippered by Captain Joseph Cunningham, anchored near the helpless *Franklin*, and both vessels made preparations to repel boarders. Their captains knew they would be fighting against tremendous odds. Cunningham had only six men in his crew; Mugford only twenty-one, including officers. Their foes would number in the hundreds.

Mugford armed his men with muskets, cutlasses, spears and pistols; he loaded his cannon with musket balls instead of round shot—and waited. In the British fleet, thirteen large boats were loaded with hardened sailors and marines, each boat containing as many men as Mugford had in the *Franklin*. Between nine and ten o'clock at night, the attacking party set out and soon neared the two privateers. Mugford heard the faint creak of oarlocks in the night and hailed, demanding to know who approached.

"From Boston," a voice answered from the dark.

"Keep off or we'll fire upon you," Mugford shouted.

"For God's sake, don't fire!" the voice answered. "We're coming aboard."

Mugford replied by firing his pistol in the direction of the approaching boats. At the signal, the *Franklin*'s broadside guns roared, dispatching a hail of musket balls into the night. Screams from the boats indicated that the deadly blast had had its effect, but before the guns could be loaded again, two or three of the boats bumped alongside, to be followed soon by others.

A wild, confused and deadly melee followed. American accounts after the action indicated that some eight or nine boats attacked the *Franklin* and that three or four concentrated on the smaller *Lady Washington*. Both privateers were defended with desperate valor in the half-hour hand-to-hand struggle that followed.

Muskets, swivels, blunderbusses were fired down into the crowded boats. Attackers who escaped this murderous fire clawed up the sides of the two vessels and were met with cutlasses, spears and clubbed muskets. As soon as a hand grasped the taffrail, a cutlass sheared it off; as soon as head or chest appeared, it was met by thrust of lance or slash of blade.

Cunningham and his six men in the *Lady Washington* put up such a desperate defense that their attackers finally sheered off. Aboard the *Franklin*, the fighting raged on with unabated fury. According to accounts of the times, two of the attacking boats were sunk by the *Franklin*'s defenders, with their crews flung screaming and floundering into the icy waters of the harbor. One last furious attempt was made to carry the little privateer, but this too was beaten back by Captain Mugford and his men.

General Artemas Ward, who had taken command of American forces in reoccupied Boston, wrote Washington on May 20 that it was believed the British had lost sixty or seventy men. "The intrepid Captain Mugford fell a little before the enemy left his schooner; he was run through with a lance while he was cutting off the hands of the pirates as they were attempting to board him, and it is said that with his own hands he cut off five pairs of theirs," Ward wrote. "No other man was killed or wounded aboard the *Franklin* . . ."

The *Franklin* was refloated with high tide the next day and made her escape, joining the rest of Washington's privateers in rounding up the British strays that continued to come in from the sea. A convoy of thirty-five transports carrying some 3,000 Highland troops had sailed for Boston about a month after the evacuation, but before knowledge of this development reached England. Storms dispersed the convoy; and, though British frigates rounded up most of the troopships later, several sailed doggedly on for Boston.

The *Lee*, *Lynch*, *Warren* and *Franklin* of Washington's little fleet had good pickings. First, they seized the troopship *Anne*; then, on June 15, they fought a spirited action with two transports, the *George* and the *Arabella*. The troopships were so stoutly defended that the privateers could not take them, but instead harried them toward Boston, now deserted by the British fleet. The skippers of the transports, thinking Boston still in British hands, sailed thankfully into harbor—only to learn their error when cannon balls from batteries ashore began to whistle past their ears. Both ships were taken, and just three days later, yet another troopship, the *Lord Howe*, fell into the clutches of the Yankee privateers.

In all, the privateers captured 354 Highland troops before they could land to fight against Washington's army, no mean achievement. The Marine Committee of Congress, not knowing quite what to do with this oddly commissioned fleet, finally ordered it disbanded in late 1777; but by that time the little schooners had taken some fifty-five prizes and had given Washington many of the resources—everything from muskets and flintlocks to powder and round shot and even winter clothing— with which to fight a war.

W VERRILL

# II

★★★★★★★

# The Privateering Life

Visions of quick fortunes to be made from privateering bewitched the minds of Americans of all classes, from farm boys unused to the sea to fishermen turned warriors and ship owners eager to transform their merchantmen into warships. By mid-1776, the Massachusetts patriot, Joseph Warren, was writing that the early successes of the privateersmen had been "sufficient to make the whole country privateering mad."

The Continental Congress issued its first privateering licenses on March 23, 1776; but Massachusetts, which was to send out some 1,000 privateers during the war, had gotten into the act some five months earlier. In all, before peace came in 1783, various governmental agencies had commissioned some 2,000 privateers, carrying an estimated 18,000 guns and some 70,000 men.

While Washington was having trouble recruiting enough soldiers to keep an army in the field, while the ships of the tiny Continental Navy found it difficult to fill

13

their crews, the "privateering mad" country took to the high seas in search of the kind of loot that would have made a pirate envious. For some, the dream of instant wealth became a reality; for many others, it led to incalculable hardships, capture, imprisonment and even death. Two of the many thousands who dared and suffered left imperishable accounts of their experiences; and from these one gets a vivid, unforgettable picture of the hazards braved by those who went privateering on seas crawling with hostile British warships.

Andrew Sherburne was a fourteen-year-old farm boy when the itch to become a bold privateersman took possession of him and he forsook the land for the sea. He enlisted first in the Continental sloop-of-war *Ranger*, which had been commanded originally by John Paul Jones. The *Ranger* in a long cruise captured nary a prize before she was lost with other American warships when the British captured Charleston, South Carolina. Young Sherburne and most of the *Ranger*'s crew managed to escape before the port fell.

Returning home, Sherburne signed aboard a new privateer, the *Alexander*, that had been built by the patriotic citizens of Portsmouth, New Hampshire, to replace the *Ranger*. The *Alexander* put to sea in December, 1780, cruised for several weeks without making a single prize, and finally returned to port to refit after her profitless battle with winter gales.

Sherburne intended to sail in her again, but a stranger whom he met on the streets of Portsmouth talked him into going aboard the fishing schooner *Greyhound* that had just been fitted out as a privateer. Sailors were in such demand at the time that ship captains employed every imaginable ruse to keep a live body aboard their craft once one had been lured there.

Captain Jacob Willis, of Kennebunk, Maine, the skipper of the *Greyhound*, filled young Sherburne's head with the most extravagant compliments and his stomach with spirituous liquor. The boy had had no intention of staying aboard the *Greyhound*, but the first thing he knew, there he was sailing aboard the schooner as she ran down to Old York, a small port nine miles east of Portsmouth. Here the officers put up at a waterfront tavern and played host to seafaring men during "a jovial evening." In the headaching dawn that followed, several of the "guests" found themselves, like young Sherburne, aboard the *Greyhound*, bound to sea on a privateering cruise.

The little warship headed for the Nova Scotia coast and, off Halifax, sighted a large ship that appeared to be a crippled merchantman. Captain Willis ran down toward her, envisioning a rich prize, but he was sadly disillusioned at almost the last moment when he discovered that the "crippled merchantman" was a British frigate playing possum. The Royal Navy wardog gave chase and was rapidly overhauling the *Greyhound* when a thick fog rolled in from the sea. Taking advantage of this obscuring blanket, the *Greyhound* changed course and managed to escape.

Leaving dangerous Halifax behind, Captain Willis took his privateer into the mouth of the St. Lawrence River. Here sail after sail was sighted, but all turned out to be other American privateers, thronging the river mouth and gulf like bees seeking honey. In disgust, Captain Willis had to content himself with seizing some miserable fishing shallops. He put prize crews aboard the two largest and ordered them back to the states.

Young Sherburne was sent aboard one of these prizes. His shallop encountered heavy weather crossing the Gulf of St. Lawrence, and she had hardly survived this when a strange sail popped over the horizon. The craft came up fast, overtaking the lumbering shallop, and Sherburne, in an account he later wrote, described what happened next:

"They soon began to fire upon us with long buccaneer pieces, into which they put eight or ten common musket balls for a charge. The first time they fired they did not strike us, but we heard their bullets whistle over our heads. The second time their charge went through the head of the mainsail, and the third time it went through the middle of our mainsail. We now heaved to. In a few minutes they were alongside of us, and twenty men sprang aboard with these long guns in their hands, loaded, cocked and primed, and presented two or three at each of our breasts without ceremony, cursing us bitterly and threatening our lives."

Sherburne and his companions expected to be killed at any moment, for some of their captors "seemed to be perfect furies." But the captain and officers of the enemy privateer that had taken them restrained their crew and set sail for Grand Bank on the Newfoundland coast.

"The wind being fair," Sherburne later wrote, "we arrived at Grand Bank before night, and almost the whole village were collected to see the Yankee prisoners. We were taken on shore and soon surrounded, perhaps by a hundred people. Among them was an old English lady of distinction who appeared to have an excellent education, and to whose opinion and instructions they all seemed to pay an especial deference."

Sherburne gave her a copy of the *Greyhound*'s privateering commission, an essential document in distinguishing a privateersman from a pirate. The English lady read the commission aloud "without interruption until she came to the clause in the privateer's letter of marque and reprisal which authorized to 'burn, sink, or destroy,' etc. Many of the people became so exceedingly exasperated that they swore we ought to be killed outright. . . . The old lady interposed, and soon called them to order. She informed them that we were prisoners of war and ought to be treated with humanity and conveyed to a British armed station. . . ."

Having escaped summary execution twice within the space of a few hours, the American prisoners were locked up for the night and left to worry about what might happen to them next. The following morning, they were prodded aboard a shallop, where they were locked in the scale-splattered hold still reeking of fish. Everything except the clothes they wore was taken from them. The shallop took them to another small port on the coast, where they were locked up again for the night; and the next morning they set out under guard on a twenty-mile march to Cape Placentia Bay. The cross-country trek was sheer torture. The prisoners' shoes had been taken from them, and their feet soon became lacerated on the rocks and stones along the rugged path. Leaving a trail of blood behind them, they finally reached Placentia, where they were locked up in the guardhouse.

Here they stayed from May, 1781, until September, when the British sloop-of-war *Duchess of Cumberland* arrived. They were put aboard the *Duchess* to be taken to St. John's, Newfoundland, where a number of Americans were imprisoned in the hold of a foul prison ship.

Their trials, as it turned out, were only beginning. On the night of September 19, the *Duchess of Cumberland* ran aground on a rocky, deserted island and was wrecked. Twenty men in her crew of 170 were drowned in the crashing seas, but Sherburne and the other American prisoners fought their way to shore.

They were marched overland again, back to the guardhouse in Placentia from which they had just come. Here they were imprisoned until the end of October, when the British sloop-of-war *Fairy* arrived and took them aboard for transfer to prison in England.

The *Fairy* was commanded by a Captain Yeo, whom Sherburne described as "a complete tyrant," an officer typical of a breed that was all too common in the Royal Navy of that brutal time. "Willis [another of the prisoners] and myself were called upon the quarter-deck," Sherburne wrote, "and, after being asked a few questions by Captain Yeo, he turned to his officers and said: 'They are a couple of fine lads for his Majesty's service. Mr. Gray, see that they do their duty, one in the foretop and the other in the maintop.' "

Sherburne protested that he was a prisoner of war and "could not consent to serve against my countrymen." He and Willis had no choice, however. They soon found that Captain Yeo took a savage, sadistic delight in having his seamen spread-eagled on the gratings and given a dozen lashes on their bare backs for the slightest offense. And so when Sherburne and Willis protested against going to battle stations, the boatswain simply flogged them until they saw their "duty."

They probably would not have survived the voyage to England except for the kind-hearted ship's carpenter. He was allowed by regulations to employ a couple of boys to help him, he told them, and he took them under his charge, sparing them further whippings.

Captain Yeo "had a number of men in irons on the whole passage to England," Sherburne wrote; and he was so heartily detested by his own crew that everyone rejoiced when he was relieved of command after the *Fairy* reached Plymouth. "Captain Yeo took leave of his ship without any ceremony of respect being shown him from the crew," Sherburne noted. "Shortly after, the new captain came on board, and was saluted with three cheers . . ."

The new skipper recognized the prisoner-of-war status of Sherburne and Willis and had them sent to Old Mill Prison, where they were confined for several months. Freed at last in an exchange of prisoners, Sherburne returned home; promptly enlisted in another privateer, the *Scorpion*; and almost as promptly, on returning from the vessel's first cruise in the West Indies, was captured again. This time, he was confined in the horror of all prison ships, the death-fouled *Jersey*, anchored off the Brooklyn shore. He was imprisoned in this noisome hulk for several weeks; then the war ended, and he was freed to return home.

He was now seventeen, and he had nothing but the clothes on his back—and his memories of shipboard and prison brutalities—to show for the three-year pursuit of his get-rich-quick privateering dream.

Dr. Solomon Drowne was more fortunate, but for him, too, privateering was no picnic. A Continental Army surgeon, Dr. Drowne was in financial difficulties at home in 1780; and so, hoping to repair his fortunes, he signed on as ship's surgeon in the tiny *Hope*, a privateer sloop mounting seven small guns and carrying a crew of only twenty men.

This cockleshell of a warship was commanded by Captain J. Munroe, and she sailed from Providence, Rhode Island, on October 3. Dr. Drowne, an educated man, kept a day-by-day diary that is the most vivid account we have of what life was like in stormy seas aboard a midget, makeshift privateer.

The *Hope* sailed in a northeaster with "drizzly, dirty weather." At sea the following morning, Dr. Drowne's landlubber's stomach began to teach him some of the horrors of a seafaring life. He wrote: "A heavy sea from the southward. I begin to be excessively seasick, but do not take my station upon the lee quarter till that side is pretty heavily manned. [Evidently, the *Hope* had a number of landlubbers in her small crew.] This is a sickness that is indeed enough to depress the spirits even of the brave."

As the *Hope* headed for the sea lanes off the New Jersey coast leading to British-held New York City, the weather became worse instead of better. The following day, Dr. Drowne noted: "Excessive sickness. Hove to. A heavy sea, with squalls of rain." On October 6: "Strong gales and squally; still lying by." On October 7, the storm was so bad it became doubtful whether the *Hope* could survive. Dr. Drowne's diary noted: "Get the topmast down. . . . Put our guns in the hold, etc. [In the] afternoon the gale becomes violent. Only one long-practiced seaman on board who says he ever knew it more tempestuous. Nail down our hatches and secure everything in the best manner possible. [We] have a hole cut through the storeroom to open a communication fore and aft below deck. The storm increases. Ship a sea, which carries away some of our crane iron [davits]. Get our axes into the cabin, ready to cut away the mast should there be occasion . . ."

Toward night the gale moderated, the wind shifted, the seas began to fall. The following day, October 8, the crew hung out their brine-soaked clothes to dry and found that their little vessel had weathered the storm without great damage. They continued their cruise. On October 12 they sighted the sails of a ship and a brig and gave chase, but could not come up with them. The following day they sighted a sloop and again gave chase—but night fell and they lost their quarry. It seemed as if they were jinxed, as if every prize they might have taken somehow managed to escape their clutches. Then the tables came perilously close to being turned; they almost became the quarry.

It happened on October 14. A number of sails rose up above the horizon, and they found themselves almost running into the heart of a large convoy—a whole fleet of merchantmen with a heavy escort of British frigates and ships-of-the-line. Any one of those mighty warships could have reduced the little *Hope* to a swatch of drifting splinters without half-trying, and the *Hope* hauled off and kept her distance, mooching along on the outskirts of the fleet as if she belonged there. The covering warships had so many helpless merchantmen to herd that one tiny sail more or less made little difference, and the *Hope* fortunately escaped their notice.

Now luck turned and smiled upon them. On October 15, having managed to separate themselves from the dangerous enemy fleet during the night, they spotted a lone sail. They closed with her and discovered her to be a snow—a two-masted vessel with the main- and foresails of a full-rigged ship, but with a third stubby mast carrying a trysail just abaft the mainmast. The snow hoisted English colors, and the *Hope*, crew cheering, forced her to come to and sent an armed boat crew to board her.

"She sailed from Kingston, Jamaica, upwards of forty days since, in a fleet, and was bound for New York, Captain William Small, commander," Dr. Drowne wrote. "She has ten men on board and four excellent four-pounders. Her cargo consists of one hundred and forty-nine puncheons, twenty-three hogsheads, three quarter casks and nine barrels of rum, and twenty hogsheads of muscovado sugar."

She was a valuable prize, laden with enough liquor to make all Rhode Island happy; and the problem, now that she had been taken, was to get her into port before some of those prowling Royal Navy sea dogs could interfere. The prisoners were all taken aboard the *Hope*, and two prize masters and ten men, more than half the little privateer's complement, were put aboard the snow. Then the exultant captors, towing their prize, set out for home.

Even now, even in their moment of triumph, nothing went smoothly for them. They were buffeted by strong gales—"northwest and very cold," Dr. Drowne noted. On October 17, he reported: "A squall with hail and snow comes up which splits the snow's jib to pieces. . . . Take a drink of grog, made of snow water. Very heavy squalls indeed this night, with a rough, bad sea. Obliged to cast off the dull snow and let her go her pace. . . . Sleep little."

The following day the doctor, who was now longing for land and whose stomach had not yet concluded a truce with the heaving sea, wrote unhappily: "Boisterous weather still, a tumbling sea going. Feel qualmish. . . . The wind so contrary we make but slow advance towards our desired haven."

Day after day, the stormy weather continued. "At this rate," Dr. Drowne commented gloomily, "the West Indies will bring us up sooner than Martha's Vineyard or Nantucket. . . . Have our pistols hung up in the cabin to be in readiness for the prisoners should they take it in their heads to rise upon the watch in the night."

Contrary winds and thick weather buffeted and plagued them until they became "fairly lost" and were like some ghost ship blown back and forth across the sea, having no slightest knowledge of where they were. They did not know, Dr. Drowne reported, "whether we are to the eastward of Nantucket, or between Martha's Vineyard and Block Island, or the last and Montauk Point [at the extreme eastern end of Long Island]." Finally, on October 21, six days after they had captured the snow, the weather cleared; and they found themselves, to the doctor's utter amazement and delight, in full view of Martha's Vineyard, with the broad reach of Nantucket Sound beckoning them home to Providence.

"What an excellent landfall!" the doctor exulted. "To one who has never been out of sight of land a whole day before, seeing it again is very pleasing, though after only seventeen days' deprivation. It is very disagreeable tossing about in so small a vessel at this season of the year. . . ."

They had not seen their valuable prize for days and worried about whether she had been lost or recaptured;

but as the weather cleared away, there the snow was, making in toward the headlands from the sea. The *Hope* and her prize stood up the roads toward Providence, but nature was not done with them yet. Another pea-soup fog closed down upon them, making matters difficult; but they were in off the treacherous sea now, and nothing could dampen their jubilant mood.

"Our men are in uncommon spirits," Dr. Drowne concluded. And well they might have been, for they had achieved in one short cruise every privateersman's dream: they had come home with a rich prize.

Dr. Drowne's share of the prize money solved all his financial difficulties, and he resolved never again to risk himself and his "qualmish" stomach on the inclement ocean. He went back to the Continental Army, serving as a surgeon through the rest of the war; and after peace was declared he became a professor of botany at Brown University.

# III

# Jonathan Haraden

JONATHAN HARADEN was the John Paul Jones of American privateersmen. Just as Jones was the supreme naval hero of the Revolution, so Haraden stood out above all other privateering captains, a man of incredible daring and resource, a skipper who often triumphed over odds as great as three to one.

Slender of figure, with thin sloping shoulders, Haraden had light-colored, close-cropped hair, keen blue eyes and a beaked, hawk's nose. Many men were physically more imposing, but none exceeded him in unruffled calm and instant inspiration in the heat of battle.

He was a man with ice water in his veins; a man who, like the British Navy's Lord Nelson in later years, deliberately donned his gaudiest waistcoat when going into battle, as if defying enemy sharpshooters to kill him. His composure became the rock on which his fighting crews based their confidence; and throughout the long course of the Revolution, the composure never faltered, the rock never cracked. The result was a record unrivaled by anyone, Navy captain or privateersman. Jonathan Haraden—the most famous seaman to hail from Salem, Massachusetts, that home port of great sailors—captured enemy vessels estimated to have mounted 1,000 guns. In battle after battle, he was never defeated.

Typical of the manner in which he frequently snatched victory from seemingly inevitable defeat was his murderous broadside-to-broadside duel with a heavily armed Royal mail packet. Such packets were among the more powerful private ships of the day, swift vessels ferrying the King's messages and cash to distant parts of the Empire.

Haraden was commanding his favorite raider, the swift *General Pickering*, when he encountered the Royal packet bound to England from the West Indies. The *Pickering* carried only sixteen six-pounders and a crew of forty-five men and boys; the packet mounted some twenty guns and had a crew of between sixty and eighty men. A more cautious captain would have let the packet go her own way and hunted easier pickings; but Haraden closed immediately, let loose a crashing broadside, and so touched off one of his most desperate battles.

For four glasses, four hours in modern terminology, the two vessels slugged it out. Broadside to broadside, they surged slowly across the Atlantic swells, only their topsails visible above the billowing pall of powder smoke—a grayish-white shroud that smothered the hulls below the disembodied tops; a shroud rent by angry, stabbing flashes of red as the carriage guns roared.

Powder-blackened, half-naked crews worked feverishly to load, aim and fire the guns on which their safety depended. Above them in the tops, marksmen sprayed enemy decks with musket balls as the two ships surged close, within pistol shot of each other. At times, when it seemed as if they might crash together, boarders were summoned and brandished pikes and cutlasses at each other above bulwarks that almost touched. Then the gap between the dueling warships would widen slightly, and the broadside guns would roar with renewed fury.

While round shot plowed into the *Pickering* and sent deadly splinters whirring across her deck, Jonathan Haraden, wearing a vivid scarlet gold-braided waistcoat, paced calmly back and forth, pausing at times to stand by the taffrail nearest the foe. It was a vantage point from which he could count the flashes of her broadside guns, still blazing away despite all the punishment the *Pickering* had dealt out. His privateer, Haraden knew, had taken a severe pummeling, and he could not tell how much damage his own guns had done the enemy.

After four hours of this deadly slugfest, the *Pickering* was in sorry shape. Her deck was carpeted with splinters; great rents gaped in her sails where round shot had sheered the canvas; severed ends of running rigging whipped in the air. The privateer was so badly cut up that a few more broadsides might leave her an unmanageable hulk, helpless to fight, unable to flee. Knowing he must break off the action to save his ship, Haraden calmly told his helmsman to alter course.

The guns fell silent and the pall of powder smoke shredded into drifting wisps in the breeze as the *General Pickering* drew away from the Royal packet. Once out of range, the privateer laid to, and Haraden put his crew to work, feverishly splicing running rigging, bending on new sails, clearing the decks for renewed action. All was ready when Haraden received a bit of nerve-shattering news: they were almost out of powder. They had enough for only one more broadside.

There was, it seemed, only one course to follow—flight while they still had a chance. But flight was a word to which Jonathan Haraden had not yet been introduced. His calmness unshaken, he spoke to his men in a voice that might have been envied by a father at the family breakfast table.

"Very well," he said. "One charge will be enough. Load and shot the guns."

The crew of the *General Pickering* had had occasion before to wonder about the good sense of their skipper when the lust of battle possessed him. But never had they had such reason to wonder as now. Under another commander, they might have rebelled; under most privateering captains, they wouldn't have fought the Royal packet in the first place. Under Haraden, they merely muttered as they obeyed his orders that sent them back into action.

Swiftly, the *General Pickering* ran down toward the waiting packet. Ignoring the mutterings of his men, Haraden leaped into a commanding position in the lower mizzen shrouds above the quarter-deck. He looped one arm through a backstay and swayed there, a lone and challenging figure. Every eye on both ships was upon him as the *General Pickering* closed with her foe.

The range narrowed to musket-shot distance, but not a musket was fired; the great guns were still. On both ships the crews waited, wondering, tense, attention riveted on the silent figure above them, dominating the scene.

Then across the seas went the voice of Jonathan Haraden, trumpeting an audacious, impudent ultimatum.

"I will give you five minutes to haul down your colors!" he bellowed to the British skipper. "If they are not down at the end of that time, I will fire into you and sink you, so help me God!"

His dumfounded crew stared up at him as he drew a cumbersome timepiece from his pocket. Clearly, like a referee counting over a fallen prizefighter, he began to toll off the minutes of doom.

"One . . ."

A long pause while the minute hand made its circuit.

"Two . . ."

"Three . . ."

Before he could utter "Four," the British flag fluttered to the deck in surrender. An incredibly bold psychological bluff had worked the miracle that broadsides had failed to accomplish.

A boat, quickly lowered from the *General Pickering*, raced across the narrow strip of water between the ships before the Englishmen could change their minds. An account subsequently compiled from eyewitness stories of Haraden's men says that the prize crew "found blood running from her scuppers, while the deck appeared more like the floor of a slaughterhouse than the deck of a ship. On the quarter-deck, in an armchair, sat an old Gentleman, the Governor of the island from which the packet came. During the whole action, he loaded and fired a heavy blunderbuss, and in the course of the battle had received a ball in the cheek, which, in consequence of the loss of teeth, had passed out through the other cheek without giving a mortal wound."

The man whose brazen bluff had induced a powerful Royal packet to surrender was an ardent patriot who fought throughout the Revolution from opening to closing gun. Born in Gloucester in 1745, Haraden had lived almost all his life in Salem, where his parents had moved when he was quite young. He shipped out as a cabin boy before he was in his teens; and by the time the Revolution broke out, he was an experienced mariner.

He enlisted in the Army on July 11, 1775, and was commissioned a second lieutenant in John Glover's "web-footed infantry" from which Washington had drawn the crews for his privateers. After Washington's little pioneering fleet had demonstrated the rewards to be reaped from bold ocean raiding, Massachusetts decided to create her own state navy; and on June 3, 1776, Haraden was appointed first lieutenant under Captain John Fisk of Salem, who commanded a brigantine with the ferocious name *Tyrannicide.* The *Tyrannicide* mounted fourteen guns and carried one hundred men; and under Fisk and Haraden she soon became the scourge of British commerce off the Massachusetts coast.

Ten days after Haraden joined her, she captured the British packet schooner *Dispatch,* and in the next few months five additional prizes hove to under her guns. Then, on February 20, 1777, Fisk was promoted to the command of the larger brigantine, *Massachusetts,* and Haraden became skipper of the *Tyrannicide.* Given a command of his own, Haraden began to write his name large in the seagoing annals of the Revolution.

The Massachusetts Board of War ordered Fisk and Haraden to sail in company on a cruise to the coasts of Ireland, England and France. The two captains put to sea on March 24, 1777; and on April 2 they captured the ship *Chalkley* bound from Honduras to Bristol with a cargo of mahogany and logwood. This was the first rich prize in what was to become a successful and sometimes hair-raising cruise.

The ocean lanes were crawling with British merchant ships, some separated by wind and storm from their convoys, and Fisk and Haraden snapped up the strays, as busy as a pair of foxes in the henyard. Haraden took the snow *Sally*, bound from London to Quebec, and sent her safely into Salem. On April 8, Fisk in the *Massachusetts* went off to chase a strange sail, and while he was gone Haraden located a fine prospect of his own, the 500-ton ship *Lonsdale*, three times the size of the *Tyrannicide*. Undismayed, Haraden closed with his huge antagonist, and after a broadside duel that lasted three hours, the *Lonsdale* surrendered. Haraden put a prize crew aboard her and sent her back to Boston.

Next, he snatched the brig *Eagle* and the barque *White Haven* and sent them off to America. The hunting was so good that Fisk and Haraden spent days sweeping slowly back and forth across the shipping lanes as they worked their way slowly eastward. In a brief report to the Board of War, Haraden later described their encounter with a heavily armed British convoy just two weeks after his battle with the *Lonsdale*.

He wrote that they "fell in with a fleet of 9 sail bound to the Westward, one of 60 and one of 14 Guns, British Ships of War, with 7 Transports from Plymouth for New York. Being a Fresh gale we could not bare down on them; however, finding one Brig to lay astern, we took the liberty to take her under Convoy. She had on board 63 Troops, Hessens Chussers, with their accountrement compleat."

Having dispatched the Hessians to an American prison camp, Haraden and Fisk sailed on and soon brought their cruise to hazardous climax. Fisk in the *Massachusetts* slipped into the French port of Nantes on May 21 and wrote the Board of War that he feared Haraden and the *Tyrannicide* had been captured. He reported that "on the seventeenth Instant at Nine in the Morning we gave chase to a Ship standing to the Eastward and came up fast. At three got within two miles of the ship, then saw three Sail in the N.E. bearing down to us; one of said Sail brought our chase to & hoisted English colors. I bore away and made sail from them; the Ship gave me chase. Capt. Haraden bore away also; the ship came up with us fast. At Nine at Night I haul'd my Wind; Capt. Haraden bore away before the wind. At half after nine, lost sight of Capt. Haraden and soon after, lost sight of the Ship. At ten, saw three flashes of Guns, which I suppose the Ship fired at Capt. Haraden and I am afraid the Ship took him, as I have not heard or seen anything of him since."

Fisk worried unnecessarily. Haraden, finding himself pursued by a heavy frigate, had exercised every stratagem to escape that his wily sailor's mind could devise. The *Tyrannicide*'s sails were doused with water so that the canvas would retain every breath of air; stores were brought up from the hold and pitched overboard; even the carriage guns were trundled one by one into the sea. Thus lightened, stripped of almost all of her armament, the little brigantine found the wings to outspeed the frigate and scuttled to sanctuary in the Spanish port of Bilbao.

There Haraden refitted his raider. Stores were replenished and a makeshift battery mounted, and by May 31 Haraden was back at sea, capturing the 160-ton brigantine *Trepassy*. After his return from this European cruise, Haraden made one more sweep of the seas in the *Tyrannicide*. During the winter of 1777–78 he cruised to Portugal, the Madeiras and the West Indies, sending back a steady stream of prizes. Then he became involved in a dispute with the Board of War concerning the disposition of prize money and resigned his commission. On September 30, 1778, he took command of the *General Pickering*, the privateer he was to make famous.

A group of Salem merchants had built the *General Pickering* as a letter of marque, with the idea of combining cargo-carrying with prize-taking. She was only 180 tons in size and had been designed as a brigantine, but Haraden changed her to a full-rigged ship to increase her speed. Cargo-carrying limited her armament to fourteen six-pounders during her early cruises; later, when she concentrated on privateering, two more guns were added.

In the archives of the Essex Institute in Salem, as carefully preserved as if they had come from the captain's cabin only yesterday, are the logbooks of two of Haraden's cruises. One deals with his last voyage home in the *Tyrannicide*; the other, with his first venture in the *General Pickering*. The terse day-by-day entries give a vivid picture of the daily hazards of life at sea aboard a midget warship in the Revolution.

In the *Tyrannicide*'s log of April 9, 1778, appears this brief epitaph to a seaman:

"At 5 P.M. Samuel Wylie died of Small Pox.

"At 7 P.M. Buried him."

On November 27, 1778, just ten days after the *General Pickering* had sailed from Salem for the West

Indies, she was caught in a howling Atlantic storm that shredded her sails and threatened to carry away her mainmast. Haraden's log gives this stripped account:

"4 P.M. Close-reefed topsails, double reef mainsails.

"8 P.M. Handed both top sails.

"Half past 9. Hove to Under Reeft topsails, head to the wind.

"Half past 10. Wore ship to the Eastward.

"6 A.M. Bore away. Handed the Torn Sail. It blowed a hard gale & very High Sea.

"8 A.M. More moderate. Close Reeft torn Topsails."

On January 4, 1779, a one-line entry in the log reported the capture of a schooner from Nova Scotia, and the next day a brief paragraph described how the *General Pickering* flitted through an entire British convoy, drawing the fire of a large warship. The entry reads:

"Saw a sail to windward. Got all things ready for engaging & Hove about after Her & fetched to windward of her. She fired Several Shot at us. In running for her we saw several more Sail. We run through a fleet of 11 Sails but could see no prospect of taking any of them, they had so strong a Convoy. The ship that fired at us We supposed to be a two-decker as she fired from her forecastle and quarter deck."

Haraden brought his privateer into the French island of St. Pierre on January 30. Here the guns were hoisted out, the ship heeled over and her bottom scraped of barnacles and weed, and a new mainmast stepped to replace the one damaged by the storm. Provisions and cargo were taken aboard for the return voyage, and the heavily laden *General Pickering* battled back to Salem through a succession of midwinter Atlantic storms.

Here Haraden's logs end. Later records were captured and destroyed by the British toward the end of the war, but official reports and eyewitness accounts collected from the seamen in his crews by the Salem chroniclers, Captain J. P. Felt and Freeman Hunt, preserved the details of his later and more daring exploits. One of these occurred in the fall of 1779 when the *General Pickering* battled an entire flotilla of British privateers.

The enemy squadron was led by the ship *Hope*, mounting fourteen guns, followed by the brig *Pomona*, twelve guns, and the cutter *Royal George*, twelve guns. Most captains, finding themselves outnumbered by three to one and outgunned by nearly the same margin, would have made sail to get away; but Haraden calmly surveyed the opposing fleet through his telescope and held to his course.

His crew began to murmur, but Haraden, ignoring these signs of apprehension, calmly ordered them to battle stations. Then he strolled along the deck, a lean, erect figure as serene of mien as any good citizen of Salem out for a walk on a Sunday afternoon.

"There's good prize money there, lads," he said, nodding across the seas in the direction of the enemy. "You stand to your guns and do your duty, and I will make you a little promise. We will take all three of them."

Had any other captain made such a boast, his men probably would have questioned his sanity and mutinied to save themselves. But with Haraden, one never knew. He had always made good before—and so his men stood to their guns and their duty.

The *General Pickering* held the weather gauge, and this Haraden nursed with all the skill of a master of maneuver. As long as he kept to windward, the British ships would have to beat up toward him; he could maintain position, battling one at a time as they came on, or, if he chose, he could swoop down suddenly to carry an exposed craft by boarding.

The British formed in line of battle behind their most powerful vessel, the *Hope*. As the *Hope* came within range, Haraden gave a final order to his men:

"Aim low, boys. We'll give her a few broadsides and board."

The *General Pickering*'s six-pounders exploded in a running sheet of flame, and the *Hope* staggered under the impact. Again and again, the *General Pickering*'s guns roared, and the *Hope* made only feeble response.

Sensing that this was no stout-hearted foe, Haraden plunged like a hawk. A touch of the wheel sent the *Pickering* knifing through the wall of powder smoke, sent her crunching and grinding against the hull of the enemy. Brandishing cutlasses and pistols, the Americans swarmed over the bulwarks and poured in an irresistible tide along the British deck.

In a few minutes, with hardly a blow struck, the *Hope* was taken. Leaving a prize crew aboard to keep the stunned British sailors under control, Haraden quickly cast off. The odds against him had narrowed, but they were still two to one. The *Pomona* and the *Royal George* were closing in, and should they combine to pour their broadsides into the *General Pickering*, Haraden and all his crew might still be captured.

Only a lightning stroke could save them. Knowing this, Haraden drove the *Pickering* straight at the *Pomona*. Again his gunners poured out a deadly broadside; again Haraden sent the *Pickering* boring through the shroud of powder smoke. Once more there came the grinding impact of hulls coming together, the storm of yelling boarders across the decks. And once more the demoralized British sailors threw down their arms and fled below in panic.

With two ships carried, Haraden recalled his men to their guns and headed for the sole survivor of what had appeared to be, just a few short minutes before, an overwhelmingly superior squadron. The *Royal George*'s crew, shocked by the fate of their consorts, had no stomach for battle. They turned to flee, but the *Pickering* was the swifter vessel and soon ranged alongside, her broadside guns blazing. The *Royal George* answered feebly, then surrendered. Jonathan Haraden had defied odds of three to one and had captured the entire fleet arrayed against him. It had taken just thirty minutes.

The victory was a rewarding one in more than patriotic terms. The *Pomona* alone, brought into Salem, was sold at auction on October 23, 1779, for 8,900 British pounds, the equivalent of some $50,000.

Even before Haraden's men could claim their prize money, their wily commander had lured another good-sized British privateer under his guns. Haraden himself described the incident in a letter to Timothy Pickering from Cape Henlopen, October 1, 1779. He wrote:

"I left the Capes at Sundown on Tuesday last, and at Sunrising on Wedenesday Morning I discovered Two sail to windward. The Winds being light I hove out two Draggs to keep my Ship from going ahead and made all Sail I could, as though I was running from them. They both gave Chace and at 5 p.m. they got nigh enough to discover that I was a cruising Vessel.

"They both hove about and haul'd their Wind. I

immediately hove about after them, they crowded all Sail they could and Rowed at the same time. At sundown the Wind breezed up a little and as Night came on, I kept Sight of them with my Night Glass; at 8 p.m., they parted, one stood to the Northward & the other to the Southward. I kept in chace of the largest and at 9 p.m. She Hove about, being to the Windward; as she past me I hail'd her, but had no answer. Then I gave her a Broadside, but without any effect that I could perceive; then I Tackt Ship and gave her another Broadside and hail'd her. She answered from N. York. I Order'd her to haul down the Colours, which they obeyed instantly; very peaceable people like the *Hope*, though they had 14 6 & 4 pounders and 38 men."

Such tricks and tactics dotted the career of the fighting man from Salem. Once, while he was cruising in the vicinity of Bermuda, he was annoyed by two lightning-fast Bermuda sloops. They flitted about the same sector of the ocean in which Haraden was cruising, keeping a discreet distance away from his guns while they recaptured some of his prizes.

Haraden decided to set a trap for these pesky foes who were depriving his crew and himself of their hard-earned prize money. He waited for the cover of night, then put his sailors to work to change the *Pickering* into a floating booby trap. He sent down the fore-topgallant yard and mast, altering the appearance of his ship aloft. A painted canvas screen, spread tight along the sides of the *Pickering*, hid her gunports. Drags astern reduced the raider's speed and transformed her into a lumbering-looking merchantman.

When day broke, the Bermuda sloops sighted Haraden's camouflaged warship and dashed forward, anticipating easy booty. Haraden watched them from the quarter-deck, a grim smile playing about his lips. Not until the first sloop foamed up directly under his quarter, barely a pistol shot distant, did he give his orders.

"Drop that screen, men," he shouted. "Give her a broadside!"

The canvas screen was whisked away like a false face on Halloween; the *Pickering*'s gunports gaped ominously—and in that instant, a broadside belched death and destruction at the smaller Bermuda privateer. The tricked enemy did not wait for a second deadly dose from those well-served guns. They threw down their arms and surrendered.

The second privateer was some distance away when this happened, and Haraden decided to continue his deception in the hope of luring her, too, into his trap. He ordered the British ensign bent to the halyards above the Stars and Stripes, giving the impression that the first sloop must have taken the "fat merchantman." The second Bermuda skipper, who had been too far off to observe what happened accurately, was eager to claim his share of the booty; and so he drove ahead as fast as he could—and ran his sloop beautifully under the waiting guns of the *General Pickering*.

Successes such as these would have been enough to distinguish any captain, but the most dramatic episode in the career of Jonathan Haraden was yet to come. In the spring of 1780, the *General Pickering* was loaded with a cargo of sugar and sailed for Bilbao, a favorite Spanish rendezvous for American privateers in European waters. Haraden had a new and somewhat green crew. This, combined with the fact that the *General Pickering* was so heavily laden she was not her usual swift self, made him decide to waste no time in cruising, but to head directly for port to get rid of his cumbersome cargo.

As a consequence, the voyage was uneventful until May 29, 1780, when the *General Pickering* encountered a British privateer mounting twenty guns. The *Pickering* was still carrying only fourteen, and Haraden had a crew of only forty-seven men and boys. The odds against him, however, were less than they had often been, and he put up a desperate battle. After an hour and forty-five minutes of broadside dueling, the Englishman, badly cut up, decided he had had enough and sheered off in search of easier prey.

A few days later, tacking into the Bay of Biscay, Haraden encountered an even more formidable adversary. This was the British privateer *Golden Eagle*, carrying twenty-two guns and a crew of sixty. Night was just falling when the *Golden Eagle* was sighted, and Haraden, audacious as ever, ordered all sail made in chase.

It was a black night, the kind in which sea and sky blend into one inky mass and objects, looming up suddenly out of the darkness, play tricks upon the eyes and assume weird dimensions. Haraden relied upon this distortion to help him; he reasoned that the *General Pickering*, foaming up so confidently out of the night, could well appear at least twice her real size. Eager to foster this delusion, he grabbed a speaking trumpet.

"Ship ahoy!" he bellowed. "This is an American frigate of the largest size. Strike your colors, or I will sink you with a broadside."

The British captain, evidently just an ordinary man whose limited imagination could never conceive of such audacity, accepted the threat as genuine and struck his colors on the spot, without a shot being fired.

John Carnes, of Salem, was put aboard the *Golden Eagle* as prize master, and the English captain was rowed, a prisoner, to the *General Pickering*. Only when he reached her deck did he discover his error. Only then, too late, did he learn that he had surrendered so meekly to a ship barely two-thirds his size.

Trailed by the *Golden Eagle*, the *General Pickering* set course once more for Bilbao. The two ships were near the port on the morning of June 3 when they sighted a large vessel coming out of the roads toward them. She carried a vast spread of canvas and was obviously twice the size of the *General Pickering*. The captured British skipper of the *Golden Eagle* stared at the headsails of the stranger with the eye of a practiced mariner and broke into a smile. Observing this reaction, Haraden remarked:

"I gather you recognize that sail, sir. Could you tell me what ship is that?"

"Gladly," beamed the Englishman. "That is the *Achilles*, one of the most powerful privateers ever to sail out of London. She mounts forty-two guns and carries a crew of one hundred and forty men."

"Is that so?" murmured Jonathan Haraden, like a man only mildly impressed.

The British captain, who had expected dismay, gaped in astonishment at Haraden's calmness. Haraden himself, eyes on the towering headsails of the approaching *Achilles*, then added a few quiet words that left the English captain completely nonplused.

"Be that as it may," he said, "and you seem sure of your information, I shan't run from her."

Boldly, the *General Pickering* stood in toward the land, ready to match her fourteen guns against forty-two; her tiny crew—ten of her men were in the prize crew aboard the *Golden Eagle*—against the one hundred and forty men on the *Achilles*. As the day advanced, the wind died away, and the vessels were virtually becalmed. The *Achilles*, with her taller masts and larger spread of canvas, held the fading breeze longer than the *General Pickering*. Slowly she crawled across the water toward Haraden's prize, which she finally brought under her guns and easily recaptured.

Then the wind died completely, and the opposing vessels rocked gently on a nearly lifeless sea.

Word of the impending naval battle had spread along the coast, and by sunset thousands of spectators blackened the Spanish cliffs and headlands. Through the night, the expectant crowd swelled until it was estimated that a hundred thousand persons clung to vantage points along the coast or put out in small boats to get closer to the scene of action.

The disparity in size between the *General Pickering* and the *Achilles* made the outcome seem inevitable. One eyewitness, Robert Cowan, wrote that "the *General Pickering* in comparison to her antagonist looked like a longboat by the side of a ship."

Aboard the "longboat" an air of incredible self-confidence prevailed. Haraden, cool, calm, supremely self-assured, communicated his spirit to his men—never more so, perhaps, than when he turned to his first officer and said:

"I'm going below and get a little rest. Call me if she tries to close."

If their captain could sleep so undisturbed, what was there for his sailors to worry about? And sleep soundly he did. When a breeze came up with the dawn and the *Achilles* got under way, Haraden was found so soundly and blissfully asleep that he had to be shaken from his slumber.

"He calmly rose and went on deck as if it had been some ordinary occasion," a contemporary account says.

Ordering the *General Pickering* cleared for action, Haraden went forward and addressed the sixty prisoners from the *Golden Eagle*. With his own crew depleted, he had barely enough men to handle the sails and work the guns. He needed recruits, and as so often happened in the Revolution—a war marked by frequent changing of sides and allegiance—he sought them in the ranks of his captives.

The exact words Haraden used have not been preserved, but he must have been eloquent as he stressed a dual theme. He urged the British sailors to join their American brethren in a fight for liberty, and at the same time he tempted them by promising a full share of prize money to those who joined him. This prospect, considering the odds against the *Pickering*, couldn't have looked very promising, but so convincing was Haraden that a British boatswain and ten men stepped forward, volunteering their services.

His crew thus strengthened, Haraden made a final tour of the deck, talking quietly to his men.

"She's bigger than we are, lads," he told them, "but we've beaten worse odds before. Just stand firm and ready, and we'll take her. Aim low. Don't throw away your fire."

To the marksmen with small arms in the tops and on the quarter-deck, he gave this advice: "Aim at their white boot tops."

Having completed his preparations, Haraden worked the *General Pickering* closer to shore, picking his battleground with infinite care. A series of shoals extended from the coast, and Haraden placed the *Pickering* in a narrow channel between two of them. This meant that the *Achilles*, to get at him, would have to advance almost head-on, exposing herself to a near-raking fire, with her far heavier batteries unable to bear fully upon the *Pickering*.

Along the decks of the American privateer, the crew clustered near the open gunports, making ready for the first broadside. As the *Achilles* came on, narrowing the range, the orders ran down the deck:

"Cast off tackles and breechings."

"Seize the breechings."

"Unstop the touch-hole."

"Ram home wad and cartridge."

"Shot the gun-wad."

"Run out the gun."

"Lay down handspikes and crows."

"Point your gun."

"Fire!"

The seven six-pounders in the *General Pickering*'s broadside battery thundered, and their iron hail swept across the water to crash against the stout sides of the *Achilles*. The huzzahs with which the British had swept into action died out, and the forward guns of the *Achilles*, the only ones that could be brought to bear, roared their own deep-throated reply.

And so the battle was joined. Again and again the

*Pickering*'s guns roared, firing so fast that the crash of one broadside mingled with the dying thunderclap of its predecessor. Desperately the British captain tried to drive his ship through the deadly storm, hoping to close and board so that he could carry the *Pickering* with the overwhelming tide of superior manpower.

But Jonathan Haraden was too experienced a sea fighter to let himself be trapped. He kept maneuvering the *Pickering* between the shoals, kept forcing the *Achilles* to approach head-on, kept his guns battering her as she tried to close. Through it all, he stood in his favorite position—by the rail of the quarter-deck on the side nearest the enemy. Round shot and musket balls flew past, and he seemed to take a perverse delight in their ominous winging. It was a demonstration that so impressed his crew that one of them wrote years later: "All the time he was as calm and steady as amid a shower of snowflakes."

Though Haraden stood untouched, unharmed, the iron storm that swept across the *Pickering*'s decks took its inevitable toll. One round shot carried away the head of the British boatswain who had volunteered for battle; eight of the crew were wounded. Still the doughty men of Salem manned their guns and continued to pour an accurate fire into the towering sides of the man-crowded *Achilles*. For two hours, the British captain endured the unequal contest, trying vainly to board his elusive foe. Finally, despairing of ever closing with the *Pickering*, he ordered his ship swung broadside to the American privateer in the narrow lane of deep water. There at last the *Achilles*'s mightier armament was brought to bear, and the battle raged to a fierce climax.

For forty-five minutes more, the ships dueled, broadside to broadside, three guns thundering on the *Achilles* to every one on the *Pickering*. These were crushing odds; yet, for the Americans, there were some compensations. The *General Pickering* was so heavily laden that she sat low in the water and was hard to hull, while the high-sided *Achilles* loomed over the gun sights, an ideal target. Shot after shot from the *Pickering*'s guns crashed through the hull of the British privateer, tearing great gaps near her waterline. Still the stubborn British battled on. And now the Americans faced a new crisis. They were running short of round shot.

Haraden, typically, was undismayed by the discovery that he would soon be without cannon balls to fire at his huge foe. Ever the master of eleventh-hour improvisation that so often turns defeat into victory, he now made a characteristic decision. If round shot was running low, he would use something else.

"Load with crowbars," he shouted to his men.

They obeyed, and the next broadside from the *Pickering* showered the *Achilles* with a deadly hail of these crude, powder-propelled javelins. This novel rain of crowbars accomplished what round shot had failed to do. The *Achilles* had taken a fearful battering. Her hull was so badly riddled that, if she fought on, she might sink; her rigging was so cut up that soon she might not be able to flee. Then, from the skies, the crowbars plunged like spears, skewering many of her crew and driving some of the gunners from their battle stations. It was too much; the *Achilles* had taken all the punishment she could. Orders rang out, and the huge British privateer spread all the canvas she could carry, swung about and headed for the open sea.

Haraden, his fighting blood at fever heat, did not

care in this moment of victory that he had beaten off a vastly superior foe or that the way to safety in the port of Bilbao lay open before him. He wanted the complete and final triumph; he wanted a prize. And so he spread sail in pursuit.

The *General Pickering* in pursuit of the *Achilles* resembled nothing so much as a fox terrier chasing a Great Dane, but Haraden had no doubt about the outcome if he could just come up with his fleeing foe.

"Another share of prize money to any gunner who can bring down a spar!" he shouted.

His gun crews tried, expending the last of their round shot; but the iron balls whipped through sails and rigging and plunged into the sea without splintering a vital spar. The fleeing *Achilles*, with a mainsail described by eyewitnesses as one "as large as a ship of the line," drew rapidly ahead. Haraden, seeing he could not catch her, consoled himself by swinging around and retaking his original prize, the *Golden Eagle*.

Among the thousands who had witnessed the spectacular sea fight, none was so stunned by the outcome as the second lieutenant of the *Achilles*, who had been put aboard the *Golden Eagle* as prize master. He had questioned John Carnes about the size and strength of the *General Pickering*, and Carnes had answered truthfully. The English lieutenant had rubbed his hands in delight, anticipating a quick and easy victory for the *Achilles*. As the battle wore on and it became obvious the *Achilles* had met her match, the lieutenant's jubilation faded and he accused Carnes of deceiving him about the size and armament of the *Pickering*. Carnes smiled wryly and replied:

"If you knew Captain Jonathan Haraden as I do, you

would not be surprised at this. It is just what I expected, and I think it not impossible that the *Achilles* will be beaten off, and I shall have command of this prize again before night."

Haraden made his second officer a perfect prophet, for before nightfall the British lieutenant was Carnes's prisoner, and the *Golden Eagle* was anchored beside the *General Pickering* in the port of Bilbao.

The Spanish populace, thrilled by its grandstand seat at the amphitheater of war, made Haraden its idol and its hero. The *General Pickering* and the *Golden Eagle* anchored about a mile from shore, and before they had swung in the roads for half an hour, such a solid mass of spectator boats formed around them that, eyewitnesses insisted, it would have been possible to walk all the way to land by stepping from one boat to another. And when Haraden went ashore, the people lifted him aloft on their shoulders and bore him in a triumphal procession through the streets of the city. Later he was feted with an almost unending round of dinners and public receptions.

So sensational a victory could not help but enhance the Haraden legend, and accounts of the day insist that he sometimes triumphed without firing a shot, "just by the mere terror of his name." One such incident occurred off the Delaware Capes, where a British brig had recaptured one of Haraden's prizes before the vessel could reach Philadelphia.

A young cabin boy was in the prize crew taken as prisoners aboard the British warship. The boy was a devout hero-worshipper, convinced that Haraden could take any vessel smaller than a ship-of-the-line. Therefore, when a sail was sighted and the boy recognized the rigging of the *General Pickering*, he began to skip about the deck of the British brig.

"What's the matter with you?" an English bo'sun growled.

"That's my master in that ship, and I'll soon be with him," the boy predicted confidently.

"Your master?" asked the bo'sun. "And who the devil is he?"

"Why, he's Captain Jonathan Haraden!" cried the boy. "Don't tell me you've never heard of him! He takes everything he goes alongside of, and he will soon have you."

This prediction was relayed to the captain of the brig, who promptly had the boy brought aft for questioning. There, on the quarter-deck of the hostile warship, the cabin boy launched into a long recital of the epic of Jonathan Haraden. All the time he was spinning his tale, Haraden was driving to the rescue under every scrap of sail the *General Pickering* could carry. Listening to the boy rave about Haraden, the British captain evidently became distracted and failed to devote his whole attention to the real business of war until it was too late.

The day was blustery, with a high wind and a choppy sea. These conditions altered the circumstances in which a ship to windward normally held the advantage, and Haraden deliberately chose to attack from the leeward side. He swept up within musket shot of the British warship, which was heeled so far over by the wind that the waves swept along her lee gunports. Any attempt to open them would bring the sea surging along the decks. The *General Pickering*, on the other hand, was not so handicapped. She was presenting her weather battery to the enemy, and all she had to do was to depress her guns to sweep the exposed deck of her foe.

"Haul down your colors or I will fire into you!" Haraden bawled.

Helpless, the British struck, and the next day their ship was anchored as a prize alongside the *General Pickering* off Philadelphia—an event that fulfilled to the letter the rash prophecy the young cabin boy had made when the *Pickering*'s headsails first came into sight.

Such triumphs, one following swiftly on another, marked the year 1780. Haraden captured a veritable fleet of enemy vessels and sent most of them safely into port, enriching the *Pickering*'s owners, himself and his crew. The ship *Rodney*, a rich prize, was sold in Salem for 90,000 pounds—about $450,000. The brigantine *Myrrh* brought 25,000 pounds, and the brigantine *Venus* 20,000 pounds—sales that give a good idea of the rich rewards of successful privateering.

Then came 1781, and the only ill-starred adventure in Jonathan Haraden's long career. Haraden sailed for the West Indies on November 16, 1780, and cut his usual swath across the busy ocean shipping lanes. Early in the new year, he recaptured a Boston vessel that had been taken as a prize by a British privateer, and he took the *Pickering* and the recaptured ship into the Dutch island of Saint Eustatius, which had been used throughout the war as a key crossroads shipping point in the Indies.

Unfortunately for Haraden, he reached this friendly port just before Admiral George Brydges Rodney and a British fleet descended upon it on February 3, 1781. Saint Eustatius quickly fell; and Haraden, his privateer and the Boston vessel were all captured.

It is not clear just how long Haraden was a prisoner,

but he was back in Massachusetts before the end of 1781. And on May 3, 1782, he took command of the 200-ton privateer *Julius Caesar*, mounting fourteen guns and manned by forty men.

In this new ship, of which he was part owner, Haraden resumed his free-roving, odds-battling ways. In June he fought a British ship of eighteen guns and a brig of sixteen for five hours. At the end of that time, the British ships and the *Caesar* were all so badly battered that action was broken off. Describing it, Haraden wrote with wry understatement that "both parties separated, sufficiently amused."

After making repairs at sea, Haraden continued his cruise to the West Indies, bringing the *Julius Caesar* into port in the French island of Martinique, accompanied by a prize, a large vessel that he had taken after another severe battle.

The return voyage to Salem in the fall of 1782 brought further rewards. The *Julius Caesar* encountered a 400-ton ship that had served as a storeship for Lord Howe; there followed the usual thundering broadside duel, then Haraden laid her close aboard and captured her. He convoyed this rich prize into Salem, arriving on December 31, 1782. And with this act, as seamen say, he swallowed the anchor; he decided to call it a career.

He went into business, establishing a rope walk in Salem where, in later years, his workmen rove most of the rigging for one of America's most famous frigates of the War of 1812—the *Essex*, in which Commodore David Porter harried British shipping in the Pacific.

Haraden was less successful as a businessman than he had been as a sailor, however. His rope walk did not prosper, and by the time he died on November 23, 1803, he was beset with financial worries. But his fame lived on, and the stories of his famous cruises were told and retold until they became imbedded in local lore.

After gathering many of these anecdotes, the local historian, Freeman Hunt, summed up Jonathan Haraden's career in this eulogistic paragraph:

"So great was the confidence he inspired that if he but looked at a sail through his glass, and then told the helmsman to steer for her, the observation went round, 'If she's an enemy, she's ours.' . . . His officers and men insisted that he was more calm and cool amid the din of battle than at any other time; and the more deadly the strife, the more imminent the peril, the more terrific the scene, the more perfect his self-command and serene intrepidity. In a word he was a hero."

# IV

★★★★★★★

# "The Dunkirk Pirate"

THE ROYAL mail packet *Prince of Orange* was bowling along off the coast of Holland on the early morning of
May 3, 1777, as if she owned the seas. One of the most
important small ships in the world, she was ferrying
King George's mail and some Royal cash and precious
cargo between Harwich on the English coast and the
ports of northeastern Europe. In her cabin, Captain
Baxter was playing the gracious breakfast host to five
passengers, four of them wealthy British merchants; and
on deck his first mate stumped stolidly about, watching
wind and sea and trim of sail.

The mate paid scant attention when, above the
tossing surface of the sea, up hove the sails of an
odd-looking lugger. Shady antecedents were written all
over her low, narrow hull and grayish cloud of lugsails.
From her appearance she was a smuggler at least—and
perhaps, if occasion offered, a pirate. However, on this
particular day, she must have been sailing with a clean

hold and a clear conscience; for, instead of hauling her wind and keeping her distance, she was coming steadily on, knifing easily through the seas, drawing ever closer to the Royal packet.

Below in the cabin, Captain Baxter clinked a morning tankard with his guests, not even aware that a strange sail was in sight. On deck the first mate paid scant attention to the approaching lugger as the *Prince of Orange* swept swiftly along in the perfect safety of these English-owned seas. The mate turned to pace the deck, and as he did so, the peaceful nautical scene was disrupted by abrupt, surprising action.

Across the narrow gap of the seas, the lugger altered course. Her helm went over; her bow stabbed directly at the packet; and a large flag with a coiled rattlesnake and the motto, "Don't Tread on Me," whipped out from her masthead. Before the astounded first mate could realize what was happening, the piratical-looking lugger came crashing alongside the packet. Grappling irons whistled through the air, bit deep into the packet's bulwarks. And a horde of armed men, spumed up from the hold of the lugger, flooded along the packet's deck.

So swiftly did it happen that the flabbergasted first mate had no time to react. He rushed to the companionway and shouted down a warning to his breakfasting captain. Captain Baxter shoved back his chair and started to rise. It was the only warlike gesture he was to make on this day of surprises.

Before he could more than get to his feet, his first mate had been shouldered aside on deck, his crew had been overwhelmed; and into the cabin, intruding on the breakfast scene, strode a strangely menacing figure.

He was a man of medium height, stockily and

muscularly built, with dark piercing eyes and gleaming black hair drawn straight back in a queue. He had a bold face in which the most prominent feature was a long hooked nose, predatory as the beak of a hawk. In one hand he held an unsheathed sword; in the other, a pistol. Flourishing the pistol, he advised the passengers to remain seated, and that Captain Baxter was his captive.

In such dramatic fashion did Gustavus Conyngham, as daring a sea raider as the Revolution produced, serve graphic notice that England's seas were no longer England's. His was a deed that would have far-reaching consequences, playing no small part in the disruption of diplomatic relations between England and France.

Conyngham was the first of Benjamin Franklin's bold captains, and he became an important cog in Franklin's wily campaign to play on the ancient animosities of French and British—and so eventually to embroil France in America's war. The seizure of the Harwich packet was soon shaking all the chancelleries of Europe. The British reacted like a swarm of bees that had just had their hive sundered; for only twice previously, in all of Britain's long brawls with the mightiest powers of Europe, had irreverent hands been laid on sacrosanct Royal packets in home water fairly crawling with British warships.

The performer of this impudent deed was an Irish-born sailor who had become a Philadelphia sea captain and had transferred his allegiance from the Old World to the New. A complete unknown when he seized the Harwich packet, Gustavus Conyngham was about to launch on a meteoric eighteen-month career that would make him the terror of the British Isles. Not even John Paul Jones himself was more feared or more hated; and

British officialdom, reacting with outrage to the seizure of the Harwich packet, branded him "the Dunkirk pirate."

Unaware of the gathering storm clouds, Conyngham in his little warship, aptly named *Surprise*, headed back toward the French coast, escorting his prize. On the way he added insult to outrage. He fell in with the 110-ton British brig *Joseph*, bound from Messina to Hamburg with a cargo of wine, lemons and oranges; snapped her up; and shepherded her, along with the *Prince of Orange*, toward the harbor mouth at Dunkirk.

Off the port Conyngham had his first brush with trouble. Two English ketches were lying in the narrow estuary, and they blundered into the way of the *Surprise*, fouling her in an apparent attempt to cripple or delay her until she could be captured by one of the ever-roving British warships. Conyngham, bounding about the deck, cursed and threatened and fought his vessel free, taking her on into port with his two prizes.

The encounter at the harbor's mouth had cost him, however. The *Surprise* had sprung a leak in the collision with the ketches, and she would have to be laid up for repairs. Days must pass before she could get to sea again, giving the British ample time to blockade the harbor mouth, waiting for her. And giving the rulers of nations time to haggle over the fate of her captain, now suddenly a pawn in the game of power politics.

The drama built up swiftly. As soon as Conyngham reached port, he sent off fast express riders carrying the Royal dispatches he had seized to the head of the American diplomatic mission in France, Benjamin Franklin in Paris. Conyngham's messengers were not the only ones racing over the roads. In Dunkirk, Conyngham had been forced to free his British prisoners since France and England were not yet at war; and, the instant he obtained his liberty, the captain of the *Joseph* had penned an indignant protest to the British consul in Ostend. That official sped the word to Paris, where the choleric, highly capable British Ambassador, Lord Stormont, received the intelligence on the evening of May 7. He lost no time. The next morning, angry and red-faced, he confronted Comte de Maurepas, the French Prime Minister, and the Comte de Vergennes, the Foreign Minister. Stormont raged that a bunch of dastardly pirates, operating with the obvious connivance of subjects of His Majesty of France, had seized two British ships, one of them a Royal mail packet. He demanded action—at once. Imprison "the Dunkirk pirate," he thundered. Seize his ship. Seize and return his prizes. All this—or war.

The French were worried. They did not want war with England—yet. And so, suave in their regrets, they yielded to all of Stormont's demands. Pretending righteous anger, Vergennes composed a scathing rebuke that almost tore the epaulets off the shoulders of the French officers in Dunkirk who had cooperated with Conyngham. Heads would roll, Vergennes threatened, if Dunkirk officials didn't see and do their duty quickly. Of course, they saw and did it.

The blow fell so quickly that it stunned Conyngham. One moment he was the hero of Dunkirk, the man who had aroused the fervor of the British-hating French by seizing a Royal packet; the next, he found himself suddenly thrown into prison, threatened with the prospect of swinging from a British yardarm as a pirate. Days passed in ominous silence. Gustavus Conyngham, in the loneliness of his prison cell, could not find out what was happening, and he had ample time to review the events that had brought him, an obscure mariner, to the dangerous notice of kings. . . .

Born in 1747 in County Donegal, Ireland, Conyngham had been little more than a tot when his parents emigrated to the colonies and settled in Philadelphia. From that port a few years later, he first went to sea as a cabin boy aboard a brig sailing in the West Indies trade. He rose from foremast hand to mate, and by the time he was in his early twenties, he was skipper of the brig, the *Charming Peggy*. In 1773 he married Anne Hockley, the daughter of a Philadelphia merchant, and two years later, when the Revolution broke out, he took the *Charming Peggy* to sea on a voyage to Holland, hoping to bring home a cargo of saltpeter, clothing and munitions.

It was a foolhardy gamble. The *Charming Peggy* was a coastal brig, too slow and sedate a lady for a blockade runner. Taking her through the Channel, clouded by the white sails of British warships, Conyngham managed to impersonate a wallowing British merchantman so successfully that he excited no suspicion. He slipped in behind Texel Island, loaded the *Charming Peggy* with a cargo of munitions, and made ready to sail on the hazardous voyage home. Now his troubles began. According to a narrative he later wrote, "an Irishman sailor on board, the name of Brackenridge . . . deserted & Got to Ostend, informed the British Consul of every particular. In consequence, we were stopd, arrested, a guard put on board in three days."

Conyngham, as the British were to learn before the war was over, was never a man to take imprisonment mildly. The presence of a British prize crew aboard his ship was like a challenge to him to prove his mettle; and so, seizing a favorable opportunity, he led his crew in an uprising, overpowered his captors and recaptured his vessel. Shaking out sail, he tried to get the *Charming Peggy* to sea, but at the worst possible moment the wind deserted him, and his little vessel was left wallowing in a calm in full view of British warships. Boats crammed with armed British sailors were soon pulling for the *Peggy*, and Conyngham, seeing resistance useless, ordered his own crew into the ship's boats and escaped to shore.

He made his way to Dunkirk, where he joined a growing swarm of American sailors and skippers marooned in Europe by the war. As chance would have it, the right man had come to the right spot at the right time.

Dunkirk, long the home port for cross-Channel smugglers, in this year of 1776 assumed new importance in the eyes of American commissioners in Paris, anxious to fit out sea raiders to prey on British commerce. The Continental Congress had sent Benjamin Franklin, Silas Deane and Arthur Lee abroad with this object in mind; and Franklin, having obtained a friendly and covert wink from French officialdom, had started a hunt for swift vessels that might be turned into channel raiders.

Franklin's marine agent was William Hodge, a Philadelphia merchant, and Hodge went to the smuggling haven of Dunkirk, hunting potential warships. While there, he met Conyngham, whom he had known and admired; and so in early 1777, when Hodge purchased the *Surprise*, he urged Franklin to name Conyngham to command her.

John Hancock, as President of the Continental Congress, had given Franklin a number of blank commissions. Franklin now took up one of these blank commissions and filled in Conyngham's name, making him a captain in the Continental Navy. The commission was dated—a simple detail that was to become important later—March 1, 1777.

The whole procedure, like George Washington's commissioning of his little fleet, was highly irregular; but then revolutions are not fought with the established military services available to existing governments. Technically, as with Washington's fleet, the vessels Hodge bought would be official warships, but the "regular Navy" atmosphere existed only in the person of the captain. The vessels and their crews would be essentially privateers. Except for a small number of Americans, most of the sailors would be of mixed nationalities, the sweepings of the Dunkirk docks; they were interested only in prize money and were to be so difficult to discipline that in the end, in one ill-fated episode, not even Conyngham could control them.

Commanding such an unruly brood, Conyngham took the little ten-gun *Surprise* to sea on May 1, 1777, and in just four days he returned to port, herding the Harwich packet and the captured wine brig.

Never did so short a cruise create so great an international storm. With kings, ambassadors and prime ministers debating his fate, Conyngham was stripped of all his possessions, including his March 1 commission, which was forwarded to French authorities at Versailles. The French, anxious to please the angry British, tried to persuade the American commissioners to disown the document. Had the Americans agreed, Conyngham could indeed have been declared a pirate and hanged as such.

Recognizing this, Franklin and his fellow commissioners balked. They refused to desert their imprisoned sea captain and began instead to use all their influence in an effort to spring him from jail.

The British, naturally, fought such attempts and, elated by the stand of the French ministry, felt for a time that they had really bagged, once and for all, that "pirate," Conyngham. Lord Stormont was so pleased with himself that he wrote this self-congratulation: "The Success of my application with regard to the Dunkirk pirate has been highly displeasing to Franklin and Deane. They made strong Remonstrances, but were given to understand that there are some things too glaring to be winked at." King George III himself was so overjoyed that on May 14 he wrote Lord North, his Prime Minister, suggesting that Parliament be informed of the fine French cooperation. The King noted with satisfaction that "the commander of the piratical vessel that seized the *Prince of Orange* packet boat is thrown into prison," and he saw this as "strong proof" that "the Court of Versailles mean to keep appearances." So confident were the British that they ordered two sloops of war to sail to Dunkirk to bring Conyngham and all his crew back to England for trial—and, presumably, for hanging.

The battle for the black-haired head of the imprisoned sea rover mounted in intensity on the highest levels of state. While Conyngham languished in the Dunkirk jail, contending secret services intrigued, and the tug-and-haul for his life was carried to the very summit—even into the boudoir of France's beautiful Queen, Marie Antoinette herself.

France at the time was honeycombed with spies. Lord Stormont, the British Ambassador, employed a small army of informers to such good effect that he usually knew what was going to happen before it happened. One of the most important agents on his payroll was Dr. Edward Bancroft, sometimes known as Dr. Edwards, who served as Franklin's secretary and secretly funneled information to Paul Wentworth, one of Stormont's key go-betweens. Bancroft was well aware of the strenuous efforts Franklin was making to save Conyngham. The wise old American philosopher and inventor had cut an amazing swath among the ladies of the French Court; and he did not hesitate now, while his adversary, Lord Stormont, used the regular diplomatic channels, to employ the feminine influence that he had often found to be more persuasive in the affairs of men. Bancroft, watching his master's maneuverings, sat down late in May and wrote a confidential report that must have come as a shock to his sanguine British employers. "Lord Stormont has the ear of the Comte de Vergennes," he wrote, "but Franklin has the Queen on his side, and she will do what he says."

Conyngham, in prison, had no idea that he had become such a *cause célèbre*, a man whose plight tugged at the heartstrings of the Queen herself, but he soon became aware that a more favorable breeze was fanning his personal affairs. He was released from military confinement and given free run of the prison. He was permitted to receive any visitors he wished. And soon, before those British sloops of war could arrive to take him back to England for trial, he was quietly released, free once more to roam the streets of Dunkirk.

No timing could have been more propitious. For William Hodge had a new raider almost equipped, almost ready to go to sea.

She was a cutter of 130 tons, originally named the *Greyhound*. Larger and swifter than the *Surprise*, she had the typical rig of a speedy channel smuggler, one tall mast stepped well forward, carrying a great spread of sail, and a straight-running bowsprit. Hodge fitted her out to carry fourteen six-pounders and a crew of 106 men.

The British quickly sensed their danger. Dunkirk crawled with Lord Stormont's spies. They frequented the waterfront grog shops; they drank and ate and slept with many of the sailors who were soon to form part of Conyngham's crew. They followed Conyngham everywhere he went. The stocky sea captain could not venture out upon Dunkirk's streets without a shadow at his heels. He came to know and recognize some of these shadows, and he took at times an almost boyish delight in leading them a merry, night-long chase through the Dunkirk bars.

Conyngham's success in his brief cruise in the *Surprise* had made him a local celebrity, and even amateur volunteers in the spying business spotted his sturdy figure and determined countenance on the Dunkirk streets and reported on what they saw. The skipper of an English fishing smack, for instance, notified the Harwich postmaster of his discoveries, and that worthy forwarded the intelligence to London. He reported that a "cutter which is painted blue and yellow, which was built for the smuggling trade and reported to be a fast sailor," was about to put to sea under the command of that "daring pirate," Conyngham. Lord Stormont, awakening to the fact that "the pirate" he thought he had laid by the heels was escaping his clutches, was furious. He lodged an apoplectic protest with French authorities. Blandly pretending astonishment, the French promised solemnly to "investigate."

In this duel and counter-duel of intelligence, Conyngham and Hodge were just as aware of Stormont's maneuvers as he was of theirs. They knew that a cover was needed to give French authorities the chance to pretend ignorance, and so they arranged a devious camouflage. They "sold" the cutter to a man named Richard Allen—most conveniently, an Englishman. Hodge and Allen then put up a bond assuring the French authorities that the cutter was not about to sail on a privateering cruise. Oh, no indeed. She was bound for Bergen, Norway, with a cargo of lumber. The French, keeping perfectly straight faces, accepted this as gospel, and on July 16, 1777, the little craft, appropriately renamed the *Revenge*, pulled away from her wharf in Dunkirk.

Only a skeleton crew was aboard, but in the outer roads this deficiency was rectified. The *Revenge* came up into the wind; another vessel pulled alongside; and across the bulwarks, dark eyes flashing, his crew from the old *Surprise* at his heels, leaped Gustavus Conyngham. There followed moments packed with furious action. While the two vessels rocked gently against each other in the harbor tides, Conyngham and his men worked like stevedores transferring arms and ammunition to the *Revenge*. Then, at last, fully supplied for a cruise, they shook out sail and headed for the open sea.

Not yet were they in the clear. Stormont's spies had kept such hawklike watch on Conyngham that they hadn't been deceived for a minute about the pretended "lumber" voyage to Norway. Conyngham himself later wrote:

"A vessel in disguise in dunkirk peers to give Signals on our going out & Was executed & answered in the offing by their ships of War . . ."

Hardly had the *Revenge* cleared the harbor before she was, in Conyngham's words, "attacked, fired on, chased by several British frigatts, sloops of War & Cutters."

The swift little cutter, with Conyngham cracking on every stitch of sail she could carry, made a dash for the open sea and quickly showed her heels to the British fleet. Pursuing round shot plunged hissing into the waves farther and farther astern. The hulls of the chasing warships dropped slowly, sullenly below the horizon. Gustavus Conyngham was on the loose. The fox was in the barnyard. . . .

Not since the days of the Vikings of old had such terror swept the coasts of the tight little isle. Gustavus Conyngham, the hated "Dunkirk pirate," struck with lightning swiftness, flitted away, struck again. Soon his name was a dreaded household word in almost all of England. British ship captains hardly dared to stick bow out of port to make the short crossing of the Channel. Coastal towns were in a constant panic. Nobody knew what "the pirate" might do next, when he might land and come swaggering up the street of some port town, burning and pillaging as he went.

The fact that Conyngham was no Bluebeard—that never yet had he committed a single atrocity—registered not at all with the panic-stricken Britons, unaccustomed as they were to having their very coasts at the mercy of an enemy raider. Conyngham was so daring, so elusive, so unvaryingly successful that his deeds encouraged the free, wild play of the imagination. Nothing, it seemed, was impossible for him; nothing should be put beyond him.

The legend began building just a few short days after he had slipped the *Revenge* through the cordon of pursuing British warships off Dunkirk. On July 21, almost under the very nose of a lumbering British ship-of-the-line, he seized a large schooner, the *Happy Return*. The next day, still playing his dangerous game of tag with the frustrated British warship, he pounced upon the brig *Maria*. Both of these prizes were valuable ships that Conyngham would have liked to send into port, but he had barely time to set them afire, leaving them blazing furiously as he fled with the *Revenge* out of range of the pursuing warship's irate guns.

His third capture, on July 26, was more fortunate. The *Revenge* at last had shaken off her tormentor, and she was alone on the sea when she overhauled the brig *Patty*, not far from the British coast. The prize was nowhere near so valuable as the two that Conyngham had had to burn, but Conyngham was getting tired of seeing all his profits going up in smoke. He should reap some reward from his triumphs, and he began to consider how this could be done. Finally, he ordered the captain of the *Patty* brought before him.

He remarked conversationally that the *Patty* was a fine brig, but unfortunately her cargo was worthless to him. He would have to burn her unless, of course, her owners would be willing to pay a handsome ransom for her release.

The British captain, not wanting to see his vessel go up in flames, assured Conyngham that the owners would be glad to pay. This settled, they haggled about price, and it was finally agreed that Conyngham would release the

*Patty* upon the payment of 630 British pounds, then worth about five times that sum in dollars.

"But how will you get the money? How can it be done?" the British captain asked.

Very simply, the daring Conyngham told him. When night fell, he would take the *Revenge* in close to shore, lower a boat and land the captain. As soon as he had the money, the captain would return to the waiting boat and bring it off. Then Conyngham would free the *Patty*. If the captain tried to play him false, he warned sternly, the *Patty* would be burned.

The British captain agreed to everything; he was too eager to get his brig back to think of double-crossing his menacing captor. He landed, got the money, hurried back—and by dawn Conyngham was well out to sea again, almost out of sight of land.

Before noon, he was off in pursuit of another strange sail—one that, though he could not know it at the time, was to kick up a new storm in the chancelleries of the world in which his name was already, depending on the viewpoint, both famous and infamous.

The new chase turned out to be the brig *Northampton*. The *Revenge* came up on her fast and brought her to with a warning shot across the bow. The prize, as Conyngham quickly discovered, was a rich one. The *Northampton*'s papers showed that she was heavily laden with a valuable cargo of hemp and iron. Scanning the horizon, Conyngham found that, for once, no British warships were in sight, and he determined to put a prize crew aboard the *Northampton* and send her off for a French port. Twenty-one men were sent aboard the prize, and the two vessels parted company.

Unfortunately, shortly after the *Revenge* had disappeared over the horizon, a British warship overhauled the *Northampton,* recaptured her and sent her into Yarmouth. There the British discovered that sixteen of the twenty-one men in the captured prize crew were French. The nationality of these sea fighters was regarded by the British as proof positive of French perfidy, and once more Lord Stormont bombarded the French Foreign Office with furious protests and threats of war. Once more the French tried to defuse the issue and gain time. Foreign Minister Vergennes put on a good show of indignation. He reprimanded the officials in Dunkirk. He ordered Hodge arrested and thrown into the Bastille (he was soon released) for filing false papers about the *Revenge*'s destination, for, wrote Vergennes righteously, "it is a serious matter to lie to a King, which he hath done."

At sea Conyngham went his swashbuckling way, unaware of this new international squall, unaware that the stratagems involved in fitting out the *Revenge* had earned his friend Hodge a taste of the Bastille. All that stretch of sea between England and the continent, so long regarded by British sailors as practically their private preserve, was now the happy hunting ground of Gustavus Conyngham and his ceaselessly prowling raider. For two months he kept the coasts of Britain and Scotland in constant turmoil. He swept north to the Baltic, then south again through the Straits of Dover and into the "Irish Channel & Western Ocean." Everywhere he went he took prizes, burning and sinking most, sending just the more valuable into port. Everywhere he went he acted with the kind of incredible boldness that creates its own surprise and furnishes its own protection.

Typical of his forays was his descent upon the

coastal town of Lynn. Silas Deane told about it in a letter to a friend on August 23, 1777. "Our last accounts are," Deane wrote, "that they [Conyngham and his men] appeared off the town of Lynn, and threatened to burn it unless ransomed, but the wind proving unfavorable, they could not put their threats into execution." Only a fortunate shift of wind apparently saved Lynn, but Conyngham's audacity left a scar that was itself like a casualty of war on British minds. Not in the memory of living man could Britons recall a raider who had threatened their coasts with such bold impudence.

Leaving the terror-stricken east coast of England behind him, Conyngham pressed on into the Irish Channel, where he brought his cruise to a resounding, prize-laden climax. The seas off the Irish coast seemed literally swarming with fat merchantmen waiting to be snapped up. One after another, the *Revenge* ran them down. Twelve richly laden ships she snatched from their owners, manned and sent off to Spanish ports. This final spurt of furious prize-taking left Conyngham and his men exhausted and reduced the *Revenge*, still in hostile waters, to an almost helpless state. She had been at sea so long she was running short of water and provisions. She had manned so many prizes that she had only thirty men and boys left in her crew. In this short-handed state, she met the first angry thrust of a raging westerly that came roaring across the "Western Ocean" to batter the coasts of the British Isles.

Conyngham turned his keen sailor's face into the wind, sniffed the first stiff blasts, sensed the first angry thrusts of the rapidly rising seas, and knew that the *Revenge*, in her weakened condition, was in dire trouble. The sensible thing to do, the only thing to do, would be to duck into some coastal port and take shelter until the storm had passed. But the trouble with this remedy was that all the coastal ports were British.

Deciding he had to take the risk, Conyngham put the *Revenge* before the wind and raced the white-capped, snarling seas for the English coast. The nearest safe anchorage was the little port of Ravenglass on the coast of Lancashire. Hounded by the westerly blustering at her heels, the little *Revenge* came tearing in from the hostile ocean, bobbed like a cork through the harbor's mouth, then glided under easy sail to a sheltered anchorage. Conyngham stripped her of sail, snugged her down to ride out the gathering blasts, and then took a slow, surreptitious look around him.

What he saw was decidedly disquieting for the skipper of the most hated Continental raider on the English coasts. Just like the *Revenge*, a number of other vessels had sought haven in the harbor. Coastal snows, sloops, a couple of oceangoing brigs, they made up a small fleet lying at anchor and waiting for the storm to pass and the seas to subside. But this wasn't all, not nearly all. There was in Ravenglass one ship whose high sides and tall sweeping masts towered over all the others. Conyngham looked at her and recognized her at a glance for what she was—a powerful British frigate. The double tiers of guns along her sides were housed now, the ports closed, but Conyngham knew that at the first breath of suspicion, those ports could be dropped, the powerful guns run out. He knew that a single heavy roundshot from any one of them, striking home, could blast the *Revenge* out of the water like an eggshell.

Fortunately, the crews of the other ships were busy snugging down to ride out the storm, and nobody paid any attention to the *Revenge*. Every ship in port accepted her for what she appeared to be, a storm-driven trader like themselves, and no one on the merchant ships, no one on the deck of the British frigate, had the faintest suspicion that the sea fox for whom the whole Royal Navy was hunting had come boldly in and hunkered down amid this flock of storm-tossed pullets.

So the storm passed. The wind blew itself out. The seas subsided. And the sheltering merchantmen began to break out sail and head for the open ocean to resume their voyages. Conyngham, carrying out his masquerade, made sail with them; with them, he headed out through the harbor's mouth, just one more little merchantman in a fleet of merchantmen. Behind him, the menacing frigate lay at anchor, her guns still securely housed, her officers not one whit wiser than they had been when the *Revenge* bobbed into the anchorage at Ravenglass.

At sea again, Conyngham took stock of his situation. It was still critical. The *Revenge* had sprung her bowsprit in the buffeting she had taken before she made port; food was short, and she was almost out of water. Obviously she was in no shape to risk the stormy crossing to friendly ports on the continent. She would have to repair and revictual. But where could this be done on hostile coasts?

Conyngham considered and decided his best chance lay in Ireland. Taking the *Revenge* well out to sea, he circled the Irish coast, not raising the land again until he came off the little harbor of Kinehead on the far northwest shore. Kinehead was little more than a smugglers' and fishermen's haven. Its harbor was unfortified; no warships lay at anchor or disturbed its waters with their patrol. Bringing the *Revenge* in, Conyngham told the townspeople a harrowing story of his experiences in the recent storm. He put his seamen to work repairing the damaged bowsprit, and he bargained for water and provisions. All the time, he kept one eye on the sea, dreading the appearance of a sail that might herald an enemy cruiser. But no sail appeared. The townsfolk of Kinehead appeared unsuspicious, and in twenty-four hours Conyngham had the *Revenge* in shape to sail again.

"We got Watter, very little else to be got there," he later wrote. "The little we Got, paid them their own price . . ."

Once more at sea, the *Revenge* quickly lost herself in the ocean wastes. Sometime later a Flemish dogger (a bluff-bowed, two-masted sailing vessel) returned to her home port from a voyage to Iceland with intelligence that once more raised the blood pressure of Lord Stormont. The Flemish captain reported that he had spoken to Conyngham at sea in the first week of September. The "pirate" had given him a package of letters and two valises to be forwarded to the American commissioners in Paris. At the time, Conyngham had two prizes with him and appeared to be heading for a French port.

Learning this, Stormont once more stormed before Vergennes. And once more the French Foreign Minister reacted with appropriate diplomatic amazement and shock. What Stormont told him was really terrible, Vergennes agreed, and he issued orders on the spot that Conyngham should be arrested the moment he set foot on French soil.

This was an indiscretion that Gustavus Conyngham had no intention of committing. Having already tasted the penalties of French diplomacy in his sojourn in Dunkirk prison, he was determined not to risk a repeat performance. He had sent all of his last prizes, not into France, but to the Spanish ports of Corunna, Ferrol and Bilbao, and in late September he ended his cruise by putting into Bilbao himself.

Even in this friendly port, Conyngham was beset with troubles. His crew's term of enlistment had expired, and no funds were available to pay them off. The men threatened to mutiny, and only the fortunate arrival of a prize that was sold for enough to satisfy their claims averted violence. Most of the foreign seamen left the ship the instant they got their money, and the *Revenge*'s crew was reduced to a mere skeleton when William Hodge boarded her.

"All our seamen had left the cutter but the New England seamen . . . ," Hodge wrote. "When I went on board, there were a greater number of prisoners than our own men, and its being an open port, I wonder they did not take the vessel from our people. After my going on board with six men as a reinforcement, there was still danger, but thank God, we brought her safe into Bilbao . . ."

Never did puny force stand in more startling contrast to achievement. Conyngham's warship was a fourteen-gun one-masted cockleshell; yet the effects of his far-ranging raids had been literally stunning. No sea raider in generations had so devastated British shipping, or sheltered in British ports, or brashly endeavored, like the Vikings of old, to hold up for ransom an entire coastal town like Lynn. "In a word," wrote Silas Deane, "Cunningham [sic], by his first and second bold expeditions, is become the terror of all the eastern coast of England and Scotland, and is more dreaded than Thurot was in the late [Seven Years'] War."

Such was the terror of Conyngham's name, indeed, that at one time, according to a contemporary account, forty sail "lay at anchor cooped up in the Thames" waiting for convoy before daring to venture out. Marine insurance rates soared fantastically. A ten-percent fee was demanded to insure cargoes going the short seven leagues across the Channel from Dover to Calais. Cargoes for the West Indies that could have been insured for two and a half percent before the war now cost five percent if the vessel sailed in convoy and fifteen percent without convoy. And still the rates kept climbing until they finally reached a prohibitive twenty-eight percent. Under such financial pressures, British merchants began to desert the flag, refusing to ship their goods in British bottoms. Instead, they gave their business to French, Dutch and other neutral shipowners whose vessels Conyngham and other American raiders had no right to appropriate.

The raider who had caused British merchants all this anguish was soon at sea again. After refitting in Bilbao, Conyngham took the Revenge on a cruise off the Spanish and Portuguese coasts. The first of the new year found him poking his nose almost into the Straits of Gibraltar. He took seven prizes, manned and sent them off; but, unfortunately, six were recaptured by British warships. Ending this cruise, Conyngham brought the Revenge saucily into Cadiz, practically thumbing his nose at three powerful British warships then at anchor in the harbor.

This enemy force, any one of whom could have

easily reduced the *Revenge* to splinters, consisted of two frigates and the huge ship-of-the-line *Monarch*. Conyngham, with colossal impudence, decided to taunt the biggest lion of them all. He almost scraped the *Monarch*'s side as he rounded to with the *Revenge* and dropped anchor almost under his gigantic enemy's stern. The gesture was not lost on British officers aboard the *Monarch* who practically gnashed their teeth in anger and frustration. One of them in a letter to the *London Chronicle* later described their "mortification" and told how "the *Revenge*, American privateer commanded by Cunningham [sic], came swaggering in with his thirteen stripes, saluted the Spanish Admiral, had it returned and immediately got product, the Spaniards themselves carrying on board wood, water, fruit and fresh provisions; all of which we were witnesses of, as she anchored directly under our stern, within two cables length."

Conyngham was well aware that this taunting of the British dragon was a dangerous pastime. The *Revenge*, he wrote, had been prowling "seas covered by British cruzers of every description" with "orders from their Govermt to follow the *revenge* into any harbour she might be in & destroy her." According to Conyngham, the tempted captain of the *Monarch* tried to carry out these orders to the letter, disregarding Spanish authority in the supposedly neutral port of Cadiz.

"An English ship of the Line & two frigatts were lying in Cadiz on our arrival," he wrote; "in their usual & diabolick mode of Warfare had determined in the Night by their boats to set the *revenge* on fire. A Good french man on board of one of them Gave notice to the french Consul of their designe, who advised us of. Consequently was prepared for them, they did appear in the dead of the night, but took Care to Keep their distance; the spanish admirall had thiss notice & he politely offered a 74 gun ship to protect us. We acknowledge the favor, but was noways apprehensive of any danger; to the Contrary it was our wish they would make the Attempt."

Leaving the frustrated British warships behind him, Conyngham once more took the *Revenge* to sea and cruised northward along the Spanish coast. Heavy gales forced him to seek refuge in the port of Ferrol, but when the weather moderated, he put out again and cruised as far south as the Canary Islands. All along this route he snatched up more prizes. The brig *Peace and Harmony* and the brig *Betsey* were captured in the Atlantic; the snow *Fanny* off the coast of Portugal; the ship *Hope* and the brigs *Carabonnere* and *Tapley* in the very Straits of Gibraltar; the brig *Maria* off Cape Finisterre; two more brigs in the Bay of Biscay and still another in the straits. Off Cape St. Vincent, Conyngham overhauled and captured the tender of H.B.M.S. *Enterprize.* The huge ship-of-the-line was in sight on the horizon when Conyngham swooped down on her tender, and he barely had time to set his prize ablaze and escape from the long-ranging guns of the furious mother ship.

Now, at the peak of his success, there occurred an incident that was to have serious consequences. The practice of British merchants of shipping their wares in foreign bottoms, a device to which Conyngham himself had forced them to resort, now boomeranged against him. In May, 1778, the *Revenge* fell in with the Swedish brig *Henrica Sophia*, bound from London to Teneriffe. The brig was carrying an all-English cargo, but under international law Conyngham had no right to seize it. He would have let brig and cargo go, but his piratically minded crew had other ideas. On the point of mutiny, they demanded that the *Henrica Sophia* be taken as a prize. Conyngham was finally forced to yield, but he had the crew sign a statement absolving him of responsibility. "Whereas," the document read, "Captain Conyngham says that he has directions not to Insult any Neutral Flag yet the Cargo appearing so plain to be British property, we have engaged him to take her, & try her chance to America."

This seizure of the Swedish brig kicked up another diplomatic tempest. The Swedish Ambassador protested angrily to Spanish officials, and even Franklin felt compelled to denounce the seizure as "an act of piracy." British diplomats, who had been trying for months to force Spain to close her ports to the *Revenge*, seized upon the issue, and under this united pressure Spanish officialdom yielded. When Conyngham returned to previously friendly Corunna, he found the port barred to him, and only with considerable difficulty did he manage to refit the *Revenge* in a small neighboring inlet.

With the ports of both France and Spain now closed to him, Conyngham decided he had no choice except to leave European waters. And so in September, 1778, he sailed for the West Indies, ending a raiding career off the European coast that was to stand as one of the Revolution's most remarkable individual achievements. In less than fifteen months in the *Revenge*, he had taken sixty British vessels. Of these, thirty-three had been burned and sunk; twenty-seven had been manned as prizes. Though a number of these had been recaptured, the majority had made port and been sold for sizable sums— money that helped to finance the activities of the American commissioners in Paris. In fact, when John Adams was sent to Europe to join the American delegation, his traveling expenses were said to have been defrayed with money reaped from the sale of some of Conyngham's prizes.

November of 1778 found Conyngham off the island of St. Eustatius in the West Indies. Here he fell in with two British privateers laden with valuable cargoes, battled both and forced them to strike their colors. In rapid succession he took two schooners, a brig and a sloop, and brought all safely into St. Pierre. A dispatch from Martinique shortly afterward credited the *Revenge* with "an engagement off Barbadoes with a King's Cutter of 28 guns, which she pursued near the guns of the fort and which would not have escaped, had it not been for a high sea which prevented boarding her."

From the West Indies, the *Revenge*, loaded to the hatches with arms and munitions for the patriot cause, sailed at last for America. She reached Philadelphia on February 21, 1779. Conyngham had been gone from home for nearly four years.

Now his career did an abrupt about-face. The Marine Committee of the Continental Congress sold the *Revenge*. She was purchased by a group of Philadelphia merchants and fitted out as a privateer. Conyngham, as part owner, sailed in command. Cruising north along the New Jersey coast, he sighted two British privateers and tried to lure them into battle. When they avoided him, he gave chase. Off New York, a third sail suddenly popped above the horizon, the fickle wind failed and the British frigate *Galatea*, holding the breeze longer, came thundering down on the *Revenge*. "I made an effort to escape but in vain, her teeth were too many," Conyngham wrote. The fateful day was April 27, 1779. The British at last had captured "the Dunkirk pirate," but it had taken them nearly two years.

The hatred in which Conyngham was held now combined with one mischance—the circumstance of his first, lost commission—to put his life in jeopardy. During his imprisonment in Dunkirk after his first cruise in the *Surprise*, his commission as a Continental Navy captain had been taken from him and forwarded to French officials, never to be returned. Later, when he put to sea in the *Revenge*, he had been issued a second commission dated May 2, 1777, an unlikely day, since the *Surprise* actually had sailed twenty-four hours earlier. The Royal Navy, which had smarted for so long from Conyngham's depredations, contended that this discrepancy in dates showed he had not been a properly commissioned officer when he captured the Harwich packet, that he had been indeed nothing but "a pirate"; and it proceeded to treat Conyngham, now that he was at its mercy at last, with a brutality that became an international scandal.

Conyngham's captor was Sir George Collier, one of the most rabid rebel haters in the British service, and he made it clear at once that he considered Conyngham fit only to bait the hangman's noose. On Collier's orders, Conyngham was thrown into the lowest and foulest dungeon in British-held Manhattan—"the condemned room," as he wrote, "where was one person on suspicion of being concerne in a thieft, another supposed to be a spy." Here he stayed for two weeks "without the least morsel of bread. . . . Watter I had give to me. Continental prisoners found a method through the key hole of the door to convey some Necessaries of Life through, altho a second door obstructed the getting of very much."

When he was taken finally from this black hole,

Conyngham was subjected to further indignities. Two leg irons weighing fifty-five pounds, joined by two large links, were fastened to his ankles. Burdened by this weight, he could hardly hobble. He was lifted and tossed like a sack of grain into a cart, then "let to the Watter side by the hang man." Instead of being hanged from a yardarm or a gallows, however, Conyngham was put aboard the British ship *Camilla*. Still in irons, he was buried in the sweltering, stinking hold when the *Camilla* sailed for England. She reached Falmouth on July 7, and shortly afterward, a "Captain Bull came on board, shewed me & read his order from Sir George Collier. The purport of it was to keep me in close confinement to be arrived in falmouth; there put me in close confinement in pendinnis Castle. . . . On the road to the Castle Manny insults & observations by the people."

The sea rover who had terrorized the Channel coasts was reminded constantly that he was destined to hang. These vengeful mutterings aroused the Americans. Franklin, reading in the British press of the threats to Conyngham's life, wrote David Hartley, a personal friend in the British Parliament: "As I am well acquainted with the fact, I can assure you that he really had a Congress commission and I cannot believe that mere resentment, occasioned by this uncommon success, will attempt to sacrifice a brave man, who has always behaved as a generous enemy—witness his treatment of his prisoners taken in the Harwich packet and all afterwards that fell into his hands."

In America, Continental authorities took direct and drastic action. Conyngham's wife, friends and many of his fellow skippers petitioned Congress to intercede for him. Congress did. It notified Collier that it would take a life for a life if Conyngham was executed; and as proof that it meant business, it ordered a Royal Navy officer, a prisoner in Boston, put in irons.

The threat evidently had its effect. On September 29, 1779, Franklin, in a letter from Passy to a friend of Conyngham's, detailed his efforts and added: "I have been made to understand in answer that there is no intention to prosecute him and that he was accordingly removed from Pendennis Castle and put among the common prisoners at Plymouth, to take his turn for exchange. The Congress, hearing of the threats to sacrifice him, put three officers in close confinement to abide his fate, and acquainted Sir George Collier with their determination, who probably wrote to the British ministers."

When he was transferred to Plymouth, Conyngham was thrown into the dreaded Mill Prison, where more than a thousand American seamen were then confined. The prison consisted of three large buildings of stone and lime, erected on a hill outside of town and surrounded by high walls. Here, at night, Conyngham was regularly flung into "the Black Hole," the deepest pit beneath the prison walls, and for a time no one was permitted to talk to him. He existed, as he later wrote, "on rebel allowance 6 oz. beef & 6 of bread for 24 hours. The least fault, as they termed it, 42 days in the dungeon on the half of the above allowance of beef & bread—of the worst quality. Suffered a severe & cruel treatment for number of years. Dogs, cats, rats, even Grass eaten by the prisoners, thiss hard to be credited, but is a fact."

Once he was permitted the freedom of the prison, Conyngham tried to escape. His first attempt failed. A little later, on a second try, he almost succeeded. The prison physician was a man about his own height and build, clad always in a black suit. Managing to obtain a black suit, Conyngham imitated the mannerisms of the physician so perfectly that he actually succeeded in strolling past the deluded sentries unchallenged. Unfortunately, he was quickly missed and was recaptured before he could get out of Plymouth.

Flung into the Black Hole as punishment, Conyngham at once began to plot an even more difficult escape. Some fifty other Americans were confined in the dungeon with him. Under Conyngham's leadership, they managed to loosen a limestone block in the floor of their prison cell, and burrowing like moles, they dug a tunnel to a point just outside the prison walls. On a dark night they broke through the final crust, committing "treason through his majesties earth," and scrambled to freedom.

On November 18, 1779, Conyngham informed Franklin of his feat in a letter from Amsterdam.

"I have the pleasure to inform you," he wrote, "that on the 3rd instant, with about 50 of our unfortunate countrymen, broke out of Mill Prison. I brought 3 officers with me. I came by way of London, it being the safest. At London we met our good friend, Mr. Digges, who did everything in his power to serve me & all his countrymen that chance to fall in his way. Happy we to have such a man among that set of tyrants they have in that country. The treatment I have received is unparalleled. Irons, dungeons, hunger, the hangmans cart I have experienced. . . . I shall always be ready to serve my country & happy should I be able to come alongside some of those petty tyrants."

During his brief stay in London, Conyngham had a novel experience. Walking one day past a print shop, he was struck by the picture of a ferocious desperado in the window. The man was a giant, nearly seven feet tall, with tremendous shoulders, great muscular arms and a fierce countenance. Under one arm he carried a sword almost as huge as himself, and his waistband was garnished with pistols. The relatively short, stocky and by no means ferocious-appearing Conyngham chuckled as he read the legend beneath the portrait: "The Yankee Pirate, Conyngham, the arch-rebel. An Admirable likeness."

The arch-rebel, on the loose again, promptly joined John Paul Jones in the Texel. Jones, fresh from his victory over the British frigate *Serapis*, had taken command of the frigate *Alliance*, and Conyngham sailed with him through the Channel and down the Bay of Biscay to Corunna. Here he left the *Alliance* and boarded the *Experiment* for home. Unfortunately, the *Experiment* hardly got to sea before, on March 17, 1780, she was run down and captured by a British warship. Once more, after a few brief months of freedom, Conyngham found himself flung back into the hideous Black Hole of Mill Prison.

Again prison could not hold him. Again he escaped. No details of this second break have been preserved, but in June, 1781, Benjamin Franklin was writing Conyngham once more, congratulating him on his safe return to France. Conyngham himself merely noted in his journal that he went first to L'Orient and then to Nantes, where he took command of the powerful twenty-four-gun privateer *Layona*, then building. But "the day she was launched, we had the information of peace." Deprived of the pleasure of fighting once more against "the petty tyrants" who had treated him so cruelly, Conyngham sailed for home.

The rest of his life was shadowed by the mystery—and to him the tragedy—of his lost first commission. When he returned to Philadelphia, he had a certificate from Franklin attesting to his services, and he applied to Congress for back pay and expenses that he had not received. His claim was reported on favorably by the Congressional Committee of War in October, 1783, but the government, being practically bankrupt, deferred payment until later. This was the closest Conyngham ever came to getting the money due him. Yearly, until 1799, he petitioned Congress; but his first commission had been lost, the British had seized his second, and Congressional committees took the perverse view that there was nothing to show he had ever been a captain in the Continental Navy.

Twice Conyngham himself searched Paris for his vanished commission; but, failing to find it, he was finally forced to abandon his just claim. During the quasi-war with France, he commanded the armed brig *Maria*, of which he was part owner, and made several cruises, but with little success. At the outbreak of the War of 1812, though he was then sixty-five, he sought to go back to the sea and repeat the successes of his youth, but failing health forced him to abandon the attempt. He died in Philadelphia on November 27, 1819, in his seventy-second year and was buried in St. Peter's Church Yard, a stone's throw from the house in Lombard Street in which he had lived and died. In his will he bequeathed to Congress his old battle flag from the *Revenge*, "the first American flag to fly in the Channel." For some years the old flag hung behind the chair of the Speaker of the House of Representatives, but it too was finally lost, and the very memory of Gustavus Conyngham faded into the mists of history.

More than a century passed before a novel discovery wrote a postscript to the story. Captain John S. Barnes, first president of the Naval History Society, happened one day to be examining the catalogue of a Paris print-seller. His eye was caught by an intriguing item, No. 143. This was advertised as the signature of John Hancock on a piece of paper dated March 1, 1777. The Hancock signature, the date, the modest price asked, all attracted Captain Barnes, and he made the purchase. When Item No. 143 was delivered to him, it turned out to be the long-missing first commission of Gustavus Conyngham. Where it had been, what had happened to it in all those long intervening years of the French Revolution and European wars and political turmoil, remains to this day a mystery; but its discovery removed the final vestige of doubt that Gustavus Conyngham had indeed been an officer of the Continental Navy—and one of whom the Navy had every right to be proud.

# V

★★★★★★

# Nathaniel Fanning

FRANCE became America's active ally after the capture of Gentleman Johnny Burgoyne and all his army at
Saratoga in 1777. The patriots' victory over trained
British and Hessian troops stunned Britain and induced
her ancient rivals on the European continent to join the
conflict while British arms were tied down in the wilds of
America.

The entrance of France into the war changed everything for American privateersmen. No longer did they
have to worry, as Gustavus Conyngham had, about their
reception in French ports. Now every port in France was
a haven, and capable American sea captains, with their
reputation for daring, were welcomed and given command of French privateers. Before the war ended, sev-
enty-eight Dunkirk privateers, only six commissioned by
Benjamin Franklin, had sailed under American commanders. The boldest of these, a man whose exploits
rivaled those of Conyngham, was Nathaniel Fanning, a

handsome devil-may-care type who sometimes collected a kiss along with his prize money.

Fanning was born in Stonington, Connecticut, in 1755, the eldest of eight sons of Gilbert Fanning. Two of his brothers were captured while serving in privateers, and one of them, Gilbert, the second son, died while confined in the notorious *Jersey*, the hell ship of all prison ships.

Nathaniel himself was in and out of British prisons several times during the war, and it was in one extended period of liberty between captures that he became, like Conyngham before him, the terror of the British Isles. He played a hair-raising game of hide-and-seek with British warships that clustered off French ports and roamed the English Channel; he seized valuable prizes almost under their very noses, raided British seacoast towns, fought broadside duels with ships many times more powerful than his and carried them with a swarm of boarders.

His career began in misfortune. After two successful privateering cruises in the early part of the war, he signed on as a potential prize master aboard the sixteen-gun brig *Angelica* in May, 1778. The *Angelica*'s cruise lasted only five days. On May 31 she encountered the twenty-eight-gun British frigate *Andromeda*, which was taking Lord Howe home after the British evacuation of Philadelphia.

Howe, according to a narrative Fanning later wrote, harangued the American prisoners and tried to persuade them to enter "his Majesty's service." None would, and Howe upbraided them, saying: "You are a set of rebels, and it is more than probable that you will all be hanged on our arrival at Portsmouth."

There followed long months of brutality. The British

sailors stripped their captives of all their possessions, even their shoes and shoe buckles, leaving them with only a shirt and pair of breeches apiece. Confined to a British prison outside Portsmouth, Fanning saw brutal guards fire into a group of helpless captives, killing one man and wounding several. He endured for a year in this hellhole before he was included in a group of prisoners being sent to France on June 2, 1779, in an exchange for captured Englishmen. As far as Britain was concerned, his release was a great mistake, for no sooner was he free than he went back to the business of war with a vengeance.

He joined John Paul Jones in Nantes, where Jones was converting a rotting East Indiaman into the *Bonhomme Richard*, a poor imitation of a frigate. Jones made Fanning a midshipman and gave him command of marksmen in the maintop. It was a post that made Fanning one of the outstanding heroes in the historic battle between the *Bonhomme Richard* and the more powerful British frigate *Serapis*.

At the climax of the battle, while grappling irons held the two ships fast together and cannon belched muzzle to muzzle, Fanning's sharpshooters in the maintop cleared out their British counterparts in the tops of the *Serapis*. Then, unopposed, they showered the exposed deck of the enemy ship below them with hand grenades and volleys of musket balls, driving the British to the gun deck below.

Fanning and his men then crept out on the *Bonhomme Richard*'s long yardarms overhanging the British deck and fired through the open hatches. Their fusillade was so unremitting and so deadly that some of the gun crews abandoned their posts, and unused powder cartridges accumulated by the guns where they had been dropped by the powder monkeys.

At this juncture, one of Fanning's men, a Scot named William Hamilton, took a basket of hand grenades and a live match out to the end of a yardarm directly above an open hatch of the *Serapis.* He threw a grenade straight down the hatch; it exploded the abandoned powder cartridges, which went up in one running, roaring sheet of flame. Twenty men were killed in an instant; many others had the clothes burned off their bodies—and the *Serapis* surrendered.

Fanning had played such a decisive role in the action that Jones in his official report recommended him for a commission. At this stage of the war, however, the Continental Navy had been almost wiped out; and Fanning, like many other American mariners, turned to privateering. Fortunately, he had learned French from French officers imprisoned with him in Britain, and this linguistic ability now served him well.

He was appointed in late December, 1780, a young man of twenty-five, to command the fourteen-gun lugsail privateer *Count de Guichen*; but since French regulations provided that only Frenchmen could command French privateers, a Captain Anthon became the official skipper. The privateer sailed from Morlaix on March 23, 1781, and in one day off the coast of Ireland snapped up four prizes. All were ransomed in a procedure in which a hostage was taken from each vessel to be held until the owners had paid the agreed ransom price to the French privateersmen.

About noon on March 27, they sighted a large letter of marque. They could tell by studying her through their spy glasses that she was a much more powerful ship than the *Count de Guichen*. The privateer mounted only fourteen tiny three-pounders, while the British vessel carried twelve long six-pounders and two stubby carronades capable of firing eighteen-pound shot at close range. Nevertheless, Fanning and Anthon decided to attack.

Fanning ordered the French ensign and an American pendant hoisted. Then, to make certain the enemy was aware they were fighting the terrible Yankees, he ordered the drummer to take station by the foremast and beat out the strains of "Yankee Doodle" as they approached. The British fired away at long range without doing any damage, and the *Count de Guichen* kept boring in, determined to force action at close quarters. In an account he later wrote, Fanning gave this description:

"We at length came within pistol shot of her, ran under her stern, and poured our broadside into her, which raked her fore and aft and which made a confounded racket in the cabin among the crockery; and some women who were passengers on board, and were in the cabin at the time, made a dreadful screeching and crying out. This single broadside drove all the English off the quarter-deck. . . ."

Fanning attempted to board, but his privateer was sailing so fast she overshot the enemy, had to wear and come back across her forefoot. Here another crashing broadside swept the British deck from bow to stern, but this time the *Count de Guichen* suffered, too. The British fired a broadside at her as she passed, cutting away the jib halyards and bringing down the foreyard "and the drummer with it."

The privateer fell off. Thinking her crippled, the British cheered and made all sail to escape. But Fanning and Anthon had no intention of abandoning the fight.

Making quick repairs to their rigging, they brought their little privateer boiling up alongside the much larger letter of marque. Here is Fanning's description of the climax of the action:

"Being ourselves now prepared with two broadsides and men ready for boarding, I then went forward, they being within hail, and commanded them to haul their colors down, if they wished for quarters, to which they made no answer. . . . Accordingly we ran under her stern, fired our cannon into her cabin windows, luffed up under her lee and layed her aboard. At the same instant the enemy bawled out for quarters and dowsed the British flag."

The battle had lasted an hour and had ended in the capture of a 400-ton vessel bound from Bristol to the West Indies and loaded with a cargo of dry goods valued at 30,000 pounds. In addition to her crew of fifty-five, the letter of marque was carrying twenty-six outward-bound British officers and seven of their wives.

When Fanning leaped aboard, the ship's captain and an Army major and captain tendered him their swords in surrender. The women "offered me their purses, which I refused to accept of."

"One of them was wringing her hands, and lamenting the loss of her husband, who had been killed in the first of the action by one of our cannon shot which passed through his body. The other gentlemen passengers kept crowding round me, and teazing me with their outcries:—that I had killed one of his majesty's colonels. Which drew from me this reply 'Blast his majesty's colonels, I wish they were all dead, and his majesty too.' "

This sentiment, Fanning confessed, he soon realized was "uncharitable," and he apologized to the colonel's widow. But he didn't feel any apology was necessary to the men.

They headed back for France, escorting their valuable prize; but now their luck ran out. They were caught in a violent storm, lost sight of their prize, and saved themselves from sinking only by throwing overboard almost all their guns. Battered and leaking, they finally limped into Brest, where they learned that the British had retaken the ship they had fought so hard to capture.

The second cruise of the *Count de Guichen* was even more unfortunate. They took several prizes and secured ransom notes; but then, as they were heading back for Morlaix, they encountered the twenty-eight-gun British frigate *Aurora*. A stiff gale was blowing, the worst of weather for a lugger, for the frigate with her towering masts could carry a much greater spread of sail in such a wind. The chase lasted sixteen hours, but then the *Aurora* ranged alongside, and Fanning was once more a prisoner.

This time, he was well treated. He and Captain Anthon were sent to a prison in Cornwall. On their promise not to try to escape, they were allowed to leave the prison every day and roam the nearby countryside, provided they returned to sleep behind bars at night. Fanning found that this type of imprisonment had decided compensations. He later recalled:

"There were a great number of farm houses within our limits, to which we used to resort, the inhabitants of which treated us with hospitality and kindness; and where I spent many agreeable hours with the Cornish girls who were generally tolerably handsome and good company; but at the same time they were very ignorant, and credulous sometimes."

Exchanged after only six weeks, he went back to France, collected his prize money, boarded ship for America—and was shipwrecked soon after leaving port, barely escaping with his life. This disaster led him to go back to privateering to repair his fortunes. He and Captain Anthon were given dual command of a fast-sailing Dunkirk cutter named the *Eclipse*. She carried eighteen six-pounders, and they sailed in her for a six-weeks cruise in early December, 1781.

Their luck was good. On December 10 they captured two ships, ransomed one and sent the other to France. The next day, they fought a bloody action with an eighteen-gun British letter of marque and forced her to strike. Then the weather, which had been murky, suddenly cleared, and they saw an English frigate bearing down on them. They had to abandon their prize and escape.

On December 15, off Land's End, they captured two sloops and a large brigantine. The brigantine had a valuable cargo, and they put a prize crew aboard her and sent her to France. The next day, they were chased by another frigate. A shot from her bow chasers carried away their topmast. Crippled, they scuttled in close to the coast, managed to give the frigate the slip in the night, and headed back to Cherbourg for repairs.

The hazards of privateering in narrow waters almost blanketed with British warships were illustrated by their next adventure. They put to sea on December 23, but had hardly stuck bow out of port before they were chased by a British frigate. It took the *Eclipse* six hours to get clear, but the high-speed race across choppy seas had sprained her hull, and she had sprung a leak. She went back into Cherbourg for more repairs.

She sailed again two days later, and Fanning noted that they "were chased every day until the first of January, when we fell in with an English letter of marque mounting twelve carriage guns." The battle was brief. The *Eclipse* sent her boarders swarming over the bulwarks, and the English surrendered. The prize, "richly laden with English goods," was manned and sent off for France.

Now, on January 3, another furious storm howled down upon them. They were forced to dismount their carriage guns and store them in the hold while they rode out the blast under a reefed foresail. At times the raging southwesterly threatened to dash them on the rocky coast, and they had to set storm foresail and jib in an effort to claw desperately away from the threatening land. "In this gale of wind," Fanning wrote, "a great number of English vessels were driven on shore, the most of which and their crews were lost. We counted in sailing along the English coast upwards of thirty wrecks."

They put back into Morlaix, repaired the storm damage, and got to sea again in the middle of February. They found the Channel swarming with English cruisers, and they were chased constantly, not a day passing without its alarms. They managed to get clear long enough to capture a large ship laden with Irish linens off the port of Dover; and on March 6 the *Eclipse* escorted this valuable prize into Dunkirk.

Fanning was now given sole command of the privateer, her owners having found a way to dodge official regulations. He supervised her complete overhaul and signed on a crew of 110 men. Half of these were French, English, Irish, Dutch and Americans; the rest came from Mediterranean ports. About thirty—Maltese, Genoese, Turks, and Algerians—were what Fanning called "boarding men." He described them as "large, stout, brawny, well-made men," who liked to go into action stripped naked except for loincloths, long knives or dirks strapped to their waists. The sight of these heathenish-appearing, piratical-looking boarders time and again struck terror to British crews.

The *Eclipse* sailed on June 6 on a cruise that was to circle the British Isles. From the start, they took prize after prize. They captured a large brigantine laden with coal and sent her off to Dunkirk. They ran a large sloop ashore near Scarborough and set fire to her. They sank two coasting sloops, then captured a large ship laden with Irish linens and dispatched her to Dunkirk.

Their hunting carried them all the way up the east coast of England, and June 16 found them off the Orkney Islands north of Scotland. Needing vegetables and fresh provisions, Fanning sent a boat ashore and demanded supplies in the name of John Dyon, captain of his majesty's cutter *Surprise*. There was a cutter named *Surprise* in the British service at this time, and the islanders, who had rarely seen a hostile warship this far north, apparently thought Fanning was a legitimate British captain.

The boat from the *Eclipse* returned laden with "a quantity of fresh provisions," and soon other boats put out from shore, bringing "several natives" to visit "his Majesty's cutter." Fanning had trouble understanding the Scots dialect, but he managed to obtain a pilot and decided to sail into Hopes Bay. He learned that a number of fur-bearing ships from Quebec were expected in a few days and that they were usually unescorted. Eager for rich booty, Fanning decided to continue his masquerade and wait for the fur ships.

Members of his crew who could not speak English were forced to stay below decks when any of "the natives" were around, leaving Fanning and the English-speaking contingent to carry out their impersonation of Royal Navy sailors. Fanning and his men played their parts so well that they lay at anchor in the harbor for seven days without arousing the least suspicion. Then, on June 27, about 2 P.M., two strange vessels appeared, sailing along the back of the island. It was evident they intended to circle the island and make for the port in which the *Eclipse* was anchored.

"On hearing this," Fanning wrote, "I went aloft, from whence, with a spy-glass, I could plainly perceive a large ship, which had the appearance of a frigate of twenty-eight guns, and a cutter mounting fourteen guns, both having English colors flying . . ."

The *Eclipse* would be trapped and destroyed if these powerful warships gained the harbor mouth, blocking her escape; but Fanning's pilot assured him wind and tide were such that the enemy vessels could not make port that night. Given this reprieve, Fanning decided on a final audacious stroke: he would ransom the town on the threat of burning it.

". . . I ordered my first lieutenant, with a number of marines well armed, to proceed to the shore, and to lay the town under a contribution of ten thousand pounds sterling, to be executed in one hour, and in that interim to send on board three of the principal magistrates of the town, whom I was to detain as hostages until the money was paid and safely lodged on board the privateer."

These plans went awry because the lieutenant did not follow orders. The astonished inhabitants, learning that their week-long "guests" were really enemies, pleaded for fifteen minutes to consult among themselves. Disobeying his orders, the lieutenant consented, but then, "with his men, fell to plundering the inhabitants of their silver plate and other rich artickles; ravishing, or attempting to ravish, the young maidens, and committing other acts of barbarity . . ."

This conduct so incensed the townspeople that they became desperate, and a mob attacked the landing party with huge clubs and stones. The lieutenant and his men fell back to the beach, where they had the protection of the privateer's guns, and Fanning fired several of his cannon, loaded with grape shot. The townspeople fled, and the lieutenant and his men pursued. They set fire to several buildings and to all the ships in the harbor before finally coming off to the *Eclipse.*

They came on board, Fanning wrote, "bringing with them a good deal of plate and other valuable articles; also a very beautiful young girl, about sixteen years of age, very handsomely dressed, and who the lieutenant begged me to suffer him to detain on board until we arrived in France, promising, when we got there, that he would marry her. Enraged at such a proposition, and being, at first sight of this beautiful young lady, greatly prepossessed in her favor . . . and also knowing the lieutenant to be already married, I ordered him immediately to be confined below to his cabin . . ."

The girl fell upon her knees and begged Fanning not to carry her off. He tried to reassure her, but she "cried, tore her hair, and raved like a mad person." Fanning got the privateer under way and ordered a boat lowered. After writing a note to the girl's parents, assuring them that she was unharmed and had been kidnapped against his wishes, he handed the girl into the boat and ordered his men to row for shore. The inhabitants of the town, not understanding his purpose, greeted him with a shower of rocks and stones.

"However, as I landed, they retired some paces back, and stood with their arms folded across their breasts, in wonder and astonishment at our boldness. Having landed the young woman, I made bold to steal a kiss from her, which was delicious, and which she returned with earnestness, saying, 'taunky, taunky, guid mon,' and then tripped away from me with a light pair of heels."

It was now high time to get away. Under cover of night, the pilot guided the *Eclipse* out of the harbor; Fanning paid him and set him on shore. Then the little privateer fled out to sea without encountering those two dangerous English cruisers.

Almost at once, Fanning resumed his prize-taking. The day after his escape from the Orkneys, he captured two sloops, manned them and sent them off to France. The next night, he captured four more sloops, sank three, and put the prisoners who were crowded into the *Eclipse* aboard the fourth, letting them go.

The privateer now rounded to the west coast of Scotland, sank two sloops "and ran into a small harbour and came to anchor, where we got a quantity of fresh vegetables and provisions." Soon after leaving this port off the northeast coast of Ireland, they encountered two British frigates and were almost captured.

In carrying a press of sail while trying to escape, the *Eclipse* sprung the head of her mast, and the frigates, which were to leeward, began to gain rapidly. Fanning decided that only a desperate gamble would save them: he would put the *Eclipse* before the wind and try to run between the two warships.

The British ships, "standing head to head," tried to close the gap between them to prevent the privateer's escape. Fanning's helmsman became unnerved at the prospect of having to thread the narrowing lane of water between the prows of the powerful frigates, and Fanning himself seized the wheel and, steering fine, drove the *Eclipse* through the gap between the charging, stabbing bows.

"By this," he wrote, "both of them began firing into us; and they hailed us from on board both ships, which we were now abreast of, and within pistol-shot, so that the officers on deck absolutely fired their pistols into us, besides the fire of the marines and top men. A great number of their shot went through our waist and boat, stowed in the chocks upon deck; one of which went through the main boom and fell into our cabin, which weighed twelve pounds. . . .

"Several of our men were wounded, but not a man killed, nor was any of our rigging damaged, but our boom and mast had several shot through them. The wind beginning to fail, we set more sail, and night coming on got clear of both frigates."

On the first of July they encountered a large British letter of marque, several times the size of the *Eclipse*. Disdaining the odds, they attacked. Fanning wrote:

"We gave her four broadsides, when the men for boarding cried out, '*A la bordage, mon capitaine.*' (Let us board her, captain.) We then ran the privateer alongside the enemy, when the boarding men leaped on board of her."

The sight of these nearly naked, steel-wielding, howling heathens unnerved the British, who abandoned their guns and fled for safety below deck. The prize was the *Lovely Lass*, a 560-ton ship mounting twenty-four long nine-pounders and several eighteen-pound carronades. She had been bound from the island of Nevis in the West Indies to Liverpool with an exceptionally valuable cargo of sugar, rum and cotton. Putting the third lieutenant and sixteen men aboard her, Fanning started for the coast of France. He became separated from his prize in the night, was chased for two days by an English frigate, and finally brought the battered *Eclipse* into L'Orient to refit.

Three weeks later he was at sea again and heading for the Irish coast. Once more the pickings were good. On July 27 the *Eclipse* captured two vessels, one loaded with sugar and coffee, the other with bales of broadcloth and linen. Both were manned and sent to France. Two days later they captured a small Bristol sloop whose captain told them there were sixteen merchant ships waiting to sail from Cork, escorted only by a fourteen-gun man-of-war tender.

While waiting for these ships to appear, Fanning decided to replenish his provisions. He sent his first lieutenant and an armed boat crew ashore with orders to pay for everything they got. About 2 P.M. the boat returned loaded with a fat ox, "few of the fattest sheep I ever saw," geese, turkeys and fowls—and a surprise.

The surprise consisted of two unscheduled guests, the young son and daughter of the Earl of Keith.

Fanning's rascally lieutenant had met them as they were returning from a hunt; he had told them he belonged to his Majesty's cutter *Surprise*; and he had so aroused their curiosity, since they had never seen a warship, that he inveigled them aboard.

The girl wore an attractive riding habit, and "both [were] very handsome and genteely dressed," Fanning later recalled. Not averse to such attractive company, he ordered his officers who could not speak English to stay below while he wined and dined the young couple in his cabin. "We chatted awhile together, and cracked a few jokes, all was glee and mirth."

After refreshments, the guests went on deck and examined "the great guns," and when the girl said she had never heard one fire, Fanning obligingly had a cannon discharged for her. The roar startled her, and she begged Fanning not to fire any more for her benefit.

The pleasant afternoon was disrupted by a hail from the masthead. A large ship was in sight off the coast. Fanning called all hands to quarters, and the hidden non-English crewmen swarmed up from the hold. Startled, hearing so many speak French, the young guests discovered they were, in effect, prisoners aboard a hostile warship.

"My dear sir," the girl said to Fanning, "I hope you are too good to have any intentions of carrying us to France."

Her brother pleaded with Fanning to let her go, because, he said, their parents were old and would be crushed by the loss of both their children. Fanning, who never had had any intention of detaining them, ordered a boat lowered and manned, then told the pair they could go ashore whenever they wished.

The young man was so moved by this gallantry that he gave Fanning his name and address, telling Fanning that, if he ever became a prisoner again, "I might command him or his fortune."

"I was now about handing the young lady over the side," the romantic captain later recalled, "when I begged her to permit me to take one parting kiss, which she without hesitation granted; and which I thought at the time sweeter than the *Scotch kiss.*"

Having landed the youngsters, Fanning turned back to the business of war, heading the *Eclipse* out to meet the powerful letter of marque coming down the coast. They could see that she was pierced for thirteen guns on a side, and they knew these would probably be larger and more powerful cannon than the *Eclipse* mounted. Still they determined to attack.

The wind having died down toward night, they got out sweeps and rowed toward their larger antagonist.

"We soon got within reach of her guns, when she began to fire upon us; but we after this soon got astern of her, where she could only annoy us with her stern chasers. At the setting of the sun we had got close under her stern, within musket shot, and could now perceive that she had a great many soldiers aboard. We now gave the privateer a rank sheer, brought our broadside to bear upon her stern, and poured it into them, which made great confusion on board of the enemy. We repeated this several times and then rowed directly alongside of her; when the boarding men being in readiness, they jumped on board the enemy, part of whom instantly quit their quarters, on seeing a number of naked men jumping on board of them. In five minutes . . . they bawled out, 'Quarters, quarters, for God's sake!' "

The prize was the *None Such*, of Bristol. She mounted twenty-six six-pounders, had a crew of eighty-seven officers and men—and, in addition, 127 British troops bound for duty in America. The action had lasted only thirty-one minutes, but Fanning's men found fourteen dead on her deck, in addition to a number who had been thrown overboard. The *Eclipse* had lost three killed and seven wounded. Fanning put his first lieutenant and twenty-five picked men aboard the *None Such* and sent her off to France, where she arrived safely at Brest.

Fanning continued his cruise, ranging the Irish and British coasts, taking prizes as he went. He landed an armed party at night on the coast of Cornwall and brought off fresh provisions much needed for the care of his wounded men and prisoners. He captured two brigs in full sight of British ships-of-the-line and frigates lying at anchor in Torbay. Finding a brig and sloop at anchor under the guns of a small fort guarding a bay near Falmouth, he impudently took the *Eclipse* straight into the bay, silenced the fort with a few well-directed broadsides, landed and spiked the guns and brought off the fort's powder. The brig, being "richly laden," was sent off to Morlaix; the sloop, being virtually worthless, was given to the 195 prisoners Fanning had accumulated aboard the *Eclipse*.

Now came Fanning's most hairbreadth adventure. On the morning of August 11, the *Eclipse* encountered three British frigates, one of them the fifty-gun *Jupiter*, one of the fastest ships in the British Navy. The wind was blowing a fresh gale from the west-southwest, and Fanning bore away from it, packing all the sail the *Eclipse* could carry. Racing across the seas with the frigates in full pursuit, the little privateer raised another sail directly ahead—a fourteen-gun British cutter, so positioned as to cut off escape.

There was no room to maneuver. Fanning had no choice: except to bear down on the cutter and hope to put her out of action. With his crew at battle stations, he sent the *Eclipse* bowling down within pistol shot of the cutter. Both vessels let loose with their broadsides without doing each other much damage. Then Fanning rounded to, bringing the *Eclipse*'s other broadside to bear; and at his order the guns roared out. This time, the aim was better; the cutter's topmast was carried away, dragging with it a mass of rigging. She was out of action.

The *Eclipse* took to her heels once more. One of the pursuing frigates stopped to help the cutter, but the other two came on. By three o'clock in the afternoon, the *Eclipse* had outsailed all but the fifty-gun *Jupiter*, which maintained the chase some three leagues astern. Then, up over the horizon popped a whole string of sails—the British Channel fleet spread out in a line over nine miles of ocean from the east end of the Isle of Wight.

The only path of escape, with the *Jupiter* pursuing furiously close behind, lay through the entire twenty-eight warships of the British fleet, some of them powerful three-deckers. It seemed like a crazy gamble, but Fanning decided that only boldness would serve. The *Eclipse* had been built in England; she was painted to look exactly like an English naval cutter; and Fanning, the play actor, resolved to give the wheel of chance one more spin as "Captain Dyon of his Majesty's ship *Surprise*."

He sent all of his non-English speaking crewmen

below, then headed the *Eclipse* boldly for the very center of the English battle line, passing directly between two huge three-decker ships-of-the-line.

"What cutter is that?" came the hail.

"His Majesty's cutter *Surprise*," Fanning answered.

Describing the action that now unfolded, he later wrote:

"We dropped our peak, and dowsed our colors, passing these wooden castles; but did not take in a rag of sail. We had nearly got without hail, when they hallooed us to bring to. We answered ay, ay; but notwithstanding kept our course. We had now given them the slip, and meant to show them a yankee trick, by giving them leg bail. The ships of the line in the centre, fired several cannon at us, the shot of which flew considerably beyond us, passing over our heads.

"Finding that we did not bring to, three frigates, a sloop of war, and a cutter, separated from the fleet, and gave chase to us. The fifty-gun ship at the same time passed through the grand fleet, and continued to chase us. The cutter appeared to outsail either of them; and she in fact sailed faster than we did.

"Perceiving this, I ordered the man at the helm from time to time, to give our privateer a rank sheer, and ordered the drag overboard to retard her way through the water. The English cutter came up within musket shot, and began firing into us. We gave her two broadsides and cut away some of her rigging (which she hove to to repair, as we supposed). But after this she did not even attempt to follow us."

This action ended just at dusk, and the *Eclipse* soon was in the clear, except for the *Jupiter*, which continued in hard pursuit. Fanning, exhausted by the day, went below for a moment, and in his absence the helmsman in a careless moment let the *Eclipse* broach to, her sails aback. The strain was too much. The topmast snapped off and fell, carrying with it a tangled mass of rigging as halyards snapped. Fanning, back on deck, put his men to work cutting away the tangle; and, in the effort, his gunner fell off the mainboom and was lost in the "bad sea running."

The *Jupiter* now roared up under the stern of the crippled *Eclipse*, and her captain thundered through his speaking trumpet:

"Strike, you damned Irish rascal; drop the peak of your mainsail, and haul down your jib sheet to windward; hoist out your boat, and come on board his Majesty's ship."

Fanning shouted back that his boat was full of holes and would not swim. The British captain ordered him to hoist a lighted lantern at the peak and wait for a boarding party.

The *Jupiter* lay with her head to the south, the *Eclipse* alongside her, heading north. The huge frigate took in her light sails and began to lower a boat filled with sailors and marines. Fanning's officers and men considered their case hopeless and were ready to surrender, but their skipper still had one trick up his sleeve. Taking the helm himself, he ordered his men to hoist sail, then lie flat on deck.

The *Eclipse* began to draw away. The *Jupiter*, becoming aware that her "prize" was escaping, lost some time recalling and hoisting aboard the boat she had lowered. This did not prevent her, however, as Fanning wrote, from opening "a most tremendous fire upon us from all parts of the ship, and she had the appearance for a few minutes of a luminous body of fire." The two vessels were so close that several musket balls were later picked up on the deck of the *Eclipse*; others were found imbedded in her spars.

The *Jupiter* crowded on sail in pursuit, and Fanning decided that he had only one chance left. This lay in tacking to windward. The *Eclipse*, being small and easily handled, could tack much more quickly than the more ponderous *Jupiter*, and the time saved on each tack meant distance gained. But to play this game the *Eclipse*, in her first tack, would have to repass the *Jupiter*, exposing herself to another murderous broadside.

"I knew this to be the pinch of the game," Fanning wrote, "and therefore cautioned once more everybody upon deck to lie as close as possible. She blazed away at us from every part of her as we passed each other. At this moment I received a flesh wound in the leg, and another in the forehead, by a splinter, and which knocked me down, and stunned me (upon the deck) where I lay some time motionless. Several of my officers and men were wounded at the same time and some of them cried out, 'For God's sake, let us strike.' "

But Fanning staggered to his feet, seized the helm himself, and promised he would have them clear in ten or fifteen minutes. He tacked again; and as the *Eclipse* sped past the *Jupiter* once more, the huge frigate's broadside guns thundered furiously. But this time the distance had increased so much the shot barely reached the little cutter.

Piling one lightning-fast tack upon another, Fanning clawed to windward, and by daylight the *Jupiter* had lost the game, dropping down into the sea four leagues to leeward.

The *Eclipse* had thirteen men wounded but none killed. Her decks and rigging bore mute testimony to the miracle of her escape. "Our waist and boat (stowed in the chocks) were pierced through and through with eighteen pound and nine pound shot," Fanning wrote. "Our sails were also full of shot holes; not less than 750 of these last could be counted (after we got clear of the *Jupiter*) in our mainsail alone. . . ."

The obvious course, it would seem, would have been to head for safety in France after so narrow an escape. Instead, Fanning saw to the treatment of his wounded, made some repairs to the *Eclipse*—and headed back for the English coast.

The very next day, off the seaport of Rye, he captured a brig and a sloop; sent the brig off to Dunkirk with a prize crew; and put ninety-four prisoners aboard the worthless sloop and let them go. And on the following day he fought one of his fiercest battles.

It was about noon when they sighted a large sail to the windward of them, bearing down toward the coast. Fanning hove to and waited for her to come up. As she drew nearer, he could tell through his glass that she was a far more formidable vessel than the *Eclipse*. She had twelve guns in broadside and appeared to be crammed with troops.

Undaunted, Fanning doused the English colors he had been flying and hoisted the French flag. With this, the action began.

"The swaggering English, having got within cannon shot, gave us a broadside, which we returned, and the action commenced within musket shot," Fanning wrote. "The English fired briskly for about fifteen minutes, and then began to slacken. At about the same time I was wounded by a musket ball, which passed through my left leg, which bled so fast that my shoe was instantly full of blood. I took a handkerchief and bound it around the wound. . . .

"We could now hear the groans of the wounded and dying on board of the enemy, whereas we had not as yet lost a single man. In order to make quick work . . . I ordered the privateer laid alongside of the vaunting English; the naked and other boarding men, being sprung upon the yards, bowsprit, & in a full flow of spirits, and anxious for the moment to arrive when they could leap on board of the enemy.

"At length we out-manoeuvered them so much, as to run under her stern, poured our broadside into her, which raked them fore and aft, and made a dreadful slaughter of them; we luffed up under her lee, and our boarding men jumped on board of the enemy, where the conflict was bloody for about six minutes, when we gained the victory. . . ."

When the enemy "bawled out for quarters," they outnumbered Fanning's boarders by almost two to one. The prize proved to be the *Lord Howe*, a 600-ton ship that had been taken into the King's service and was commanded by a Navy lieutenant. She carried twenty-four long six-pounders and a number of shorter carronades, and she had on board at the time of the battle, in addition to her own crew of eighty-seven, 110 officers and soldiers of an English regiment that had been stationed in Ireland. Fanning had entered the battle with a crew of only seventy-two officers and men.

Despite this overwhelming British superiority in force, the *Lord Howe* had been well and soundly beaten. She had lost a major, a lieutenant and twenty-one soldiers killed among the land forces; twenty-two of her own crew had been killed; and thirty-eight sailors and soldiers were wounded. The *Eclipse* had lost twenty killed and twenty-two wounded.

The *Lord Howe* had no cargo and was not very valuable as a prize. Having no intention of trying to send her to France, Fanning transferred all his prisoners to the *Eclipse*. The weather, which had been thick and murky during the action, cleared as the transfer of prisoners was being completed; and Fanning discovered a thirty-two-gun frigate, apparently attracted by the sound of firing, bearing down upon him. There was barely time to escape. Fanning's men trundled some of the *Lord Howe*'s guns into the sea and spiked the rest. Then the *Eclipse* once more spread her wings in flight. The frigate fired several shots at her, but the *Eclipse* soon proved she was the faster vessel and left her pursuer dropping hull down into the sea.

This last battle and escape convinced even Fanning that it was time to return to port. Crippled by the leg wound, and overloaded with prisoners who might try to rise and capture the privateer at any moment, he headed for Dunkirk, ending one of the most dramatic privateering cruises of the Revolution.

The rest of Fanning's career was anticlimax. Though he was only twenty-seven, his great achievements were behind him. The *Eclipse* had seen such rough service that she was deemed no longer fit for cruising, and her owners decided to replace her with an eighteen-gun brig of a new design. They offered the command of this privateer to Fanning, whose last exploits had made him the hero of Dunkirk.

Several months must pass before the new vessel

would be ready for sea, and Fanning was anxious to get away on two counts. He wanted to take more prizes while the war still lasted, and he wanted also, by his own account, to turn aside the romantic designs of the daughter of one of the privateer's owners, a lady of means but of unprepossessing appearance.

His vehicle of escape from the threat of matrimony was a small forty-ton English-built cutter which he named the *Ranger*. This miniature menace, of which Fanning was part owner, mounted only three puny four-pounders, an armament barely large enough to awe a fishing smack; but Fanning, reckless as usual, put out into the English Channel, seeking prizes.

He soon ran into a huge convoy escorted by powerful men-of-war. Having no chance to escape, he joined the fleet, posing as an English trader. So well did he carry out the ruse that he sailed along with the convoy for three days and two nights without arousing suspicion. On the third night the weather thickened, and the commodore signaled the merchantmen to seek shelter in the nearest port, which was Rye.

Fanning took advantage of the inevitable confusion. Posing as a small pilot boat, he ran alongside ship after ship, offering to put a pilot aboard to guide them into port. The skippers were naturally glad to accept such assistance and did not discover until too late that they were welcoming aboard not a pilot but a swarm of hostile boarders. Three prizes were taken in this manner without a shot being fired, an alarm given. Fanning manned them and sent them off to France, then sneaked away into the night with the *Ranger*.

Morning found him at sea with only two inexperienced Irish lads left aboard to help with the sails.

Morning light also disclosed a large cutter bearing down on the audacious little privateer. Leaving his prizes to make port as best they could, Fanning hauled away to the north, drawing the cutter after him. He could not set more sail, because he had to handle the helm himself, and his two Irish lads "did not know how to set even the square sail and topsail." By two o'clock in the afternoon, the fourteen-gun cutter ranged alongside, and Fanning had no choice but to surrender.

A mob assembled when he was taken ashore at Dover, for the word had spread that the American raider who had posed as "Captain Dyon of his Majesty's cutter *Surprise*" had been captured. As the boat bearing the prisoners neared the quay, women in the crowd of two hundred persons showered Fanning with rocks and stones. Battered and bruised, his head swelled "to double its ordinary size," Fanning was led through the mob, with women screeching "such oaths, imprecations and threats [as] I never before heard proceed from the mouth of any human being."

Even though a prisoner again, Fanning's luck still held. He was soon included in another exchange and was back in France, ready to take command of the new eighteen-gun brig. But it was now early 1783, and peace was declared before Fanning could get to sea. In the years that followed, he became an officer in the regular Navy. He died in 1805, a victim of yellow fever, while he was in command of the naval station in Charleston, South Carolina.

# VI

★★★★★★★

# Whaleboat Warriors

BRITISH warships, troopships, supply ships and coastal cargo carriers turned the waters off the American coast white with their sails, making the inshore reaches of the Atlantic a virtual replica of the clogged English Channel. This endless flow of commerce lured some of the most daring privateersmen of the Revolution, men who defied astronomical odds and raided in the smallest craft known to war—whaleboats.

The waters of New York Harbor and the sea lanes leading to it were the prime battleground in this uneven contest. The great port became, from the moment the British seized it in 1776, the principal base for the long, determined attempt to subjugate the rebelling American colonies. It was constantly reinforced and resupplied by fleets whose numbers and power dwarfed the famed Spanish Armada that had set out to conquer England.

Almost forgotten in the mists of two hundred years is the magnitude of the British war effort. It was for its time even more remarkable than the American World War II feat of transporting armies and equipment across vast oceans for wars on foreign continents. Huge convoys under the escort of British men-of-war plied back and forth across the Atlantic. Swift rum- and salt- and sugar-laden schooners arrived daily from the West Indies. More than 150 small sloops and schooners carried the produce of Tory farms in New Jersey, Staten Island and Long Island to Manhattan, the source of the King's gold. On a single day, December 23, 1779, an immense fleet of 140 merchantmen, convoyed by Royal men-of-war, stood out homeward bound from Sandy Hook. "On this occasion," according to an eyewitness account, "our waters are said to have presented a panorama never before equaled, as this immense fleet, on a fine day and before a following wind, passed out of the Hook and spread itself out over the open sea."

Such concentrations of shipping turned the waters in and around New York Harbor into a veritable battleground. The patriots had no navy worthy of the name, no warships of any size; they had only their whaleboats— sharply double-ended craft, broad-beamed, of shallow draft, some twenty-six to thirty feet in length. They carried crews of from fourteen to twenty-four men, and their only armament was a small swivel gun mounted in the bow or stern.

The swivel was a cross between a musket and a small cannon, and it was affixed to the bow of the whaleboat on an oarlock type of mount that enabled it to swing in all directions. Depending on the size of the gun—there were many variations—swivels fired iron balls weighing from a quarter of a pound to slightly less than one pound. At close quarters, the gun could be loaded with loose lead pellets, making it a deadly weapon against a massed enemy. In addition to swivels, the whaleboatmen carried boarding pikes and muskets or duck guns; but their main reliance was on their pistols and cutlasses—and the element of surprise.

Theirs was a kind of guerrilla warfare at sea, a type of fighting for which the New Jersey coast, with its proximity to New York and its innumerable tricky inlets and shallow coves, was ideally suited. A quick dash from such havens, a sudden swarm of boarders leaping out of the night on a surprised or sleeping foe, then rapid flight with the captured prize across treacherous shoals and up winding, baffling channels where heavy warships dared not follow—such was the formula for a flea-bite warfare that sometimes drove the British to distraction.

Two dynamic leaders of the Jersey whaleboatmen became legends in their time, their feats as daring and their triumphs over great odds as notable as those of a Haraden or a Conyngham or a Fanning. These heroes of whaleboat privateering were William Marriner and Adam Hyler, both of New Brunswick, New Jersey, and their raids across the inner bay and on the sea lanes along the coast spanned the entire period of the British occupation of New York.

Marriner, who began his forays across New York Harbor shortly after the British seized the port in 1776, was a tall, large-framed man of great physical strength. Though no one would have guessed it when he roared across the bulwarks of an enemy vessel, cutlass in hand, he was by nature jovial; a big, relaxed man with a broad streak of humor in him. These were qualities that made him popular and successful in his normal vocation as a tavernkeeper and that, after the war, were to make him known as a genial host to George Washington himself.

Early in the Revolution, Marriner served as a private in the New Jersey regiment of Lord Stirling. He apparently saw some active service, but he soon left the army and established his tavern hard by the banks of the Raritan River on the outskirts of New Brunswick. His waterfront hostelry quickly became the rendezvous for whaleboatmen and an informal clearinghouse for information brought in by patriot spies and informers. From securing information to acting upon it was a short and inevitable step. It wasn't long before Marriner was planning and conducting raids at the head of the hardy whaleboatmen who were his tavern's customers.

One of his most daring forays was made on the night of June 11, 1777. The British command in New York had mounted a special drive to capture prominent New Jersey patriots. Tories who knew the patriot chiefs and were familiar with the countryside engineered raids in which they snatched prisoners from their beds and hustled them off for confinement in British prisons. The Americans had no prisoners of comparable importance to be used as pawns in an exchange, and so they determined to get some.

A raiding force to strike the Long Island shore, where many prominent Tories had their country homes, was organized under the command of Marriner and Captain John Schenck, a leader of local militia. They took twenty-six picked men in two whaleboats and set out from Matawan Creek on the southwestern shore of Raritan Bay. It was a long row across the choppy lower bay, whipped by a blustering east wind, before they struck the Staten Island shore just north of Princess Bay. Hugging the shore in the black night, they battled the angry chop until they reached the Narrows, the deep channel that separates Staten Island on the west from Long Island on the east and that connects the upper and lower reaches of New York Harbor.

They slanted across the Narrows and grounded their boats on the Long Island shore not far from the spot where the New Utrecht ferry road came down to the bay. They leaped ashore, dragged their boats into a thicket and placed a guard over them. Three pickets were stationed on roads leading down to the beach to prevent surprise, and Marriner and Schenck led the rest of their men inland on their raid.

They had drawn up a list of the prominent Tories whom they hoped to capture. Top priority was given to David Matthews, the Tory mayor of New York. Next came Miles Sherbrook, a personal foe of Marriner; the wealthy Jacob Suydam; Colonel Axtell; and Theophylact Bache, the president of the New York Chamber of Commerce, whose brother Richard had married a daughter of Benjamin Franklin.

Marching their men into the shadows of a neighborhood church, Marriner and Schenck formed four raiding parties. Each was equipped with a heavy timber for use as a battering ram. The plan was for each squad to hit a selected home at the same time. When they had taken their prisoners, they would return to the church, unite there and go back to their boats in a body.

The four parties of raiders disappeared into the night on their separate missions. At first, their luck seemed all bad. The British in New York led a gay existence, with an almost nightly round of parties; and Mayor Matthews and Colonel Axtell on this particular night were attending a night-long revel that would probably keep them in the city until dawn. Balked, Marriner led his men to the homes of others on his list.

In the Suydam home, his men found Captain Alexander Gradon, an American officer who had been captured the previous November. He had been billeted with the Suydams, waiting for exchange, and Marriner's raiders freed him and took him with them.

The other squads had even better luck. Bache was found asleep in bed and dragged away, a captive. In the nearby home of George Martense, Sherbrook was found hiding in a garret behind a large Dutch chimney, his breeches in his hands. He was hustled off to the rendezvous at the church just as he was, and there, while his captors waited for other squads to join them, he managed to struggle into his pants before being led with Bache down to the waiting whaleboats.

While the Americans hadn't captured as many Tories as they had hoped, the raid had been daring and successful—so successful that Marriner was lured into repeating it several times in the next few months. On one raid, he captured Lieutenant Forrest and Major Moncrieff, whose daughter Marguerite was to become the first love of Aaron Burr. On another, he landed at New Utrecht, seized the noted Tories, Simon and Jacques Cortelyou, and made off with specie and property valued at $5,000. All of the prisoners taken in such raids were brought back to New Jersey and subsequently exchanged for patriot leaders or officers of the Continental Army.

Marriner did not confine himself to such prisoner-gathering expeditions. Time and again he led his men against British shipping in the lower bay. On one occasion, when a fleet of small craft huddled in the cove behind Sandy Hook to seek protection from the weather, Marriner took a small whaleboat fleet across the bay and captured three sloops and an armed schooner. An adverse wind and tide forced the sloops ashore, where Marriner stripped them of cargo and gear and set fire to them. While they burned, he made off in the schooner, which turned out to have a valuable cargo. His men received $1,000 each in prize money for their one night's work.

Another cruise of Marriner's was even more remarkable. On the night of April 18, 1780, he dropped down the Raritan from New Brunswick in a single whaleboat. He had with him just nine men. They crossed the bay to Sandy Hook. Inside the tip of the Hook, protecting the anchorage in the cove, lay a powerful British guardship, a three-decker named the *Volcano*. Nearby was a saucy little brig, the *Blacksnake*. She had been fitted out as a privateer by Rhode Islanders, but had been overtaken by the British frigate *Galatea* and sent in as a prize. She lay at anchor now, supposedly untouchable under the broadside guns of the mighty *Volcano*. She drew and held Marriner's calculating eye.

Approaching through the night with the utmost stealth, the oars of his whaleboat muffled in the oarlocks, Marriner glided undetected under the stern of the *Blacksnake*. The brig was manned by a prize crew of twenty men under Captain Cornelius French, but the disparity in numbers was more than offset by the difference in alertness. French and his crew were asleep; Marriner and his men definitely were not. They swarmed in a rush over the counter of the prize; seized and disarmed the lone and sleepy lookout; battened down the hatches, imprisoning the crew in the forecastle; and stationed guards at the entrance of the after cabin. All had been accomplished in seconds, without resistance, without a sound.

Having captured the privateer, Marriner determined to bring her off. Quickly he cut her anchor cable, quietly shook out some sail. The *Blacksnake* began to move through the water, ghosting out of the anchorage. Nearby, the powerful watchdog of the British fleet slept on; the volcano did not erupt.

Daylight found Marriner and his nine whaleboatmen well out to sea, almost out of sight of land, a stout little warship under their feet and the shipping lanes leading to New York wide open for their hunting. Almost at once a plump pullet of the sea fell into their seeking hands. About 6 A.M., up from the south scudded the schooner *Morning Star*, lightly armed with swivels, but packed with a crew of thirty-three men commanded by Captain Richard Campbell.

Marriner, bold as the captain of a seventy-four, brought the *Blacksnake* ranging alongside. With his nine followers manning the eight-pounders in the little brig's broadside, there was nobody left to work the sails; but Campbell and the crew of the *Morning Star* did not know that. The *Blacksnake* looked formidable to them, and they surrendered. Once the two ships had crunched together, however, and Marriner's men started to board, the British captain saw how few they were and called on his men to fight. He and several of his followers were promptly cut down, and the rest, cowed by the fate of the others, fled below.

Marriner, who had started out the previous night with one whaleboat and nine men, now had a brig and schooner to handle and fifty prisoners to keep subdued in their holds. He knew that he had to get his prizes into port quickly before weariness overcame his men and the prisoners rose up and recaptured their vessels.

Running swiftly down the coast to get away from the heavily patrolled waters around New York, Marriner ducked in through Cranberry Inlet (now no longer in existence, then a deep cut through the barrier beach about where the town of Lavalette now stands) and brought his prizes into Toms River. There they were condemned and sold.

This was Marriner's last major victory. Shortly afterward, in another raid into Long Island, he was surprised, surrounded and captured. Paroled, he returned to his tavernkeeping in New Brunswick. From there, on April 14, 1781, just a year after his capture of the *Blacksnake* and *Morning Star*, he wrote a letter to British officials. Rumor evidently had credited him with another raid in the bay, and Marriner wanted to set the record straight.

"In a New York paper it is said I was concerned in taking a sloop," he wrote. "Such a report is without foundation. I am on parole, which I shall give the strictest attention to. She was taken by Hyler and Dickie."

This is one of the first mentions of the raider whose achievements with the whaleboat fleet were to surpass even those of Marriner.

Adam Hyler was the son of Philip Hyler, who came to New Brunswick from Baden, Germany, about 1752. Adam was born in Germany, probably about 1735. He went to sea in early youth and, according to one version, was impressed and forced to serve for a time in the

British Navy. When the Revolution broke out, he was a man of about forty and a citizen of some standing in New Brunswick. He operated his own small fleet of sloops and trading vessels and lived in comfortable circumstances in a one-and-a-half-story log-and-frame house. His first wife, Christina Auble, had died, and on November 13, 1777, he married pretty twenty-three-year-old Ann Nafey.

This is all that is known about the personal life of Adam Hyler before, in the last years of the Revolution, he burst upon the scene as an unparalleled leader of small-boat warriors. He was, by all accounts, a shorter, chunkier man than Marriner, with powerful arms and torso. He had probably been active in Marriner's whale-boat fleet, but nothing is known of these activities. His name did not begin to appear in the newspapers until after Marriner's capture and enforced retirement, but after a few early mentions, his exploits became the feature of almost daily headlines. Into one eleven-month span, beginning in October, 1781, Adam Hyler packed a lifetime of action.

The first spotty references to Hyler dot the record of the previous year. In November, 1780, he led the whale-boatmen in a successful foray along the Staten Island coast, snatching the sloop *Susannah* from her anchorage. In the spring of 1781 he and his raiding companion, Captain Dickie, evidently captured another sloop in the action for which Marriner had been incorrectly blamed. And on August 5, 1781, Hyler took a leaf out of Marriner's book by crossing to the Long Island shore in a prisoner-hunting raid. A correspondent in New Brunswick reported to the New Jersey *Gazette* in Trenton that Hyler had "marched three and a half miles into the

country, and made Captain Jeromus Lott, a Lieutenant-
Colonel of Militia, and one John Hankins, a Captain of a
vessel, prisoners, and brought them safe to New Brunswick."

These actions were little more than tune-ups for the
main events in the career of Adam Hyler. It all began
on the night of Friday, October 5, 1781. Early in the
afternoon, a patriot courier had brought word to Marriner's tavern in New Brunswick—a clearinghouse for
secret information—that a fat covey of potential prizes
nestled inside the sheltering arm of Sandy Hook. Hyler
hastily rounded up his whaleboat crews and led a tiny
armada down the tortuous shoal-cluttered Raritan. In the
van was a little sloop that Hyler had christened the
*Revenge*; trailing were two whaleboats. The tiny flotilla
reached South Amboy at the mouth of the Raritan, and
there Hyler waited for night to fall. When an inky
blackness at last shrouded shore and bay, he set out,
heading for the scene of action.

The *Revenge*, towing the whaleboats, ghosted silently toward Sandy Hook. Hyler knew that he was
challenging the most astronomical odds the whaleboatmen had ever faced. Out near the point of the Hook,
cannon rising in tiers up her black sides, lay the guardship, a powerful British ship-of-the-line. Five smaller
vessels rocked gently on the waters of the cove, secure
under the protecting flank of this behemoth. Three of the
anchored craft were merchantmen, but the other two
were armed, and either one should have been more than
a match for the *Revenge* and her whaleboats. The
smaller, a sloop, mounted a three-pounder cannon and
six swivels; the larger carried four six-pounders, two to a
side. These guns afloat were supplemented by guns

ashore, for a log redoubt, manned by Tories, squatted at the base of the Sandy Hook lighthouse, barely a half mile from the scene of impending action.

Off the anchorage Adam Hyler brought the *Revenge* up into the light wind. Like a gull, the sloop drifted, black hull blending into black water. Softly Hyler called one of his whaleboat crews to him and instructed them to reconnoiter the anchored vessels. The men departed on their mission as noiselessly as creeping cats. The leather-wrapped oars moved without a creak in their padded tholepins as the whaleboat glided slowly off into the night, leaving not the slightest ripple of a wake. Impatiently, Hyler waited for its return.

His men were gone for a long time, but when they returned, their report was encouraging. The merchantmen looked deserted; apparently, most of their crews had gone ashore for a night's revelry in the little Tory hamlet that had grown up near the log redoubt. There were men on the privateers, but their watch was lax. Hyler's whaleboatmen had nudged up almost under their counters without being detected. They had also gotten close to the mighty guardship without touching off an alarm. Nor did anyone seem to be stirring aboard her; her watch must have been sound asleep.

Listening to this report, Hyler decided to waste no more time but to swoop down on the anchorage at once. He assigned one whaleboat crew to board the three nearly deserted merchantmen. The second whaleboat would attack the smaller privateer. He and his men in the *Revenge* would attempt to take the stronger vessel.

The whaleboats stole off into the night. Hyler waited a few minutes to let them get in position; then he put the *Revenge*'s helm over and sent her coasting down upon the anchorage. Closer and closer the little sloop groped through the night toward the indistinct shadow of her foe. The shadow grew in size, began to take shape as a ship; and the *Revenge*, hardly a ripple at her forefoot, narrowed the gap to yards, to feet, to inches. Gently she bumped against the counter of the Tory craft, and in that instant grapnels swung, biting into bulwarks, welding the two vessels fast. In that instant, too, Hyler leaped for the enemy's deck, his men pouring up and over the side behind him.

The pounding feet of the boarders woke the slumbering foe. The deck watch screamed an alarm, then went down in the rush. In the forecastle, startled sailors grabbed cutlasses and pistols and tried to sally forth. Only the first few made it. Hyler and his men charged up beside the hatch, standing guard with their cutlasses and threatening to lop off the first head that showed itself. Not relishing that fate, the bulk of the crew huddled in safety below.

Seeing this, the few who had gained the deck fled aft. A couple dived overboard; the others dropped into the longboat that trailed by a painter off the stern and started to row frantically for shore. Resistance was over, the ship carried—all in the space of seconds, without the loss of a man.

Elsewhere in the anchored fleet, Hyler's whaleboatmen had struck with equal swiftness and equal success. The smaller privateer had been carried, only a few of her crew escaping in the vessel's yawl. The merchantmen had been virtually deserted. Aboard them, the whaleboatmen encountered only sleeping watches and, in the cabin of one, a mother with four children clutching at her nightclothes.

The entire fleet of five ships had been carried with breathtaking speed, but the real danger lay ahead. The Tories who had fled ashore in the longboat would give the alarm; the log redoubt would come to life; the huge cannon aboard the massive guardship would begin to thunder. Hyler and his men would have to work fast.

They did. Cargo from the captured vessels was trundled across the deck and dumped into the *Revenge* and the whaleboats. Guns, sails and cordage were swiftly plundered. As the whaleboatmen worked furiously, guns ashore began to speak. The first of the refugees had reached the log fort, and the garrison there started to blaze away with twelve swivel guns. The range was too great, the night too dark for the shots from the little popguns to find their mark and do any damage. But the noise they made was danger enough. The whole anchorage was coming to life. Out near the point that slumbering watchdog, the Royal man-of-war, was rousing at last. Lights flashed from the portholes; shouted commands rang across the water. Adam Hyler, surveying the turmoil he had caused, decided it was time to leave.

Sparing the one ship on which the woman and her four children huddled, he fired the others, shook out every rag of sail the *Revenge* could carry, and flitted toward the safety of the bay, towing his whaleboats. Behind him the pyres of burning vessels lit the sky; behind him, finally, the huge cannon of the guardship roared in throaty anger. The waters of the bay spouted and frothed with the plunging, ricocheting roundshot; but the little *Revenge* was moving fast, a ghostly shadow in the black night.

Hyler's return to New Brunswick in the brightness of day was triumphal. The New Jersey *Gazette*'s corre-

spondent reported gleefully that the tiny flotilla had
come back laden with prisoners, with sails and cordage
stripped from the captured vessels and with other booty
that included "250 bushels of wheat, a quantity of
cheese, several swivels, a number of fuzes, one cask of
powder and some dry goods."

Just eight days after this thundering prelude to a
dramatic career, Hyler with the *Revenge* and his two
whaleboats was back again, nosing around his special
happy hunting ground—the cove behind Sandy Hook.
One would have thought that the British, stung once,
would have been alert a second time, but Hyler evidently
relied on the Royal Navy's supreme arrogance and blind
faith in its own invincibility. He obviously reasoned that
the enemy would dismiss his first raid as a fluke, that
they would never imagine a whaleboat privateersman
would be audacious or foolhardy enough to strike again
in the same spot. Yet there were two schooners and a
sloop, anchored just off the lighthouse fort, practically
begging to be taken.

Hyler's second raid was a copy of the first, with a
single difference. This time it was even easier.

Only two watchmen had been left behind on the two
ships; the rest of the crews were carousing ashore. And
even the watchmen were asleep. They were surprised
and made prisoners before they could utter one startled
cry. Hyler, looking about him, realized that he had taken
three ships so swiftly and silently that no one was aware
of what had happened. And so he decided to try to bring
away all three of his prizes.

With his men in the *Revenge*, he had taken the
larger of the schooners. He assigned a whaleboat crew to
each of the other vessels. Swiftly the sails were spread

and the anchors catted, and the little fleet stood out into the bay, leaving fort and guardship blissfully asleep.

The raid had proceeded without the slightest hitch, but now trouble developed. The captured sloop proved such a dull sailer that she held back the whole flotilla; yet it was essential for Hyler to cross the bay and get behind the protecting shoals of the Raritan before dawn. The British, in an effort to combat the whaleboat raids, had armed several fast-rowing galleys with one heavy cannon apiece. One shot from the long eighteen- or twenty-four-pounder cannon these galleys mounted would demolish any craft in Hyler's fleet. Hyler had no desire to encounter such formidable antagonists in daylight while he was encumbered with prizes; and so, three miles out in the bay, he halted his little fleet and set fire to the sluggish sloop that was holding up their progress.

Flames from the burning vessel lit up the night and woke the British to the realization that some of their ships were missing. Hyler, of course, knew that the blazing sloop would stir up British patrols in the bay, but he estimated he had such a head start that he could be safely up the Raritan before they could catch him. Everything would probably have worked out just that way, too, except that the tide was falling, and off Point Comfort, at the mouth of the Raritan, the smaller of the captured schooners ran hard and fast aground on a sand bar. There was no time to refloat her, for one of the British galleys from Staten Island, alert at last to what was happening, came rushing up out of the night like an angry terrier, barking with her heavy twenty-four-pound thunderbird as she came.

Hyler's men stripped the stranded schooner of stores, sails and cordage, then set fire to her. Shepherding his whaleboats and his one remaining prize, Hyler went on up the Raritan, while behind him sailors from the British galley put out the flames aboard the stranded schooner. When high tide came, the craft was refloated and towed back to the Hook. As for Hyler, he reached New Brunswick with his prize, described as "a remarkably fine, fast-sailing Virginia-built pilot boat, mounted with one 4-pounder."

These two successful raids, just eight days apart, made Hyler an instant hero among the patriots. He was not, however, a man to rest content with past achievements; just eleven days after his successful foray into the anchorage behind the Hook, he was back again, harrying the Tories. The *Gazette* correspondent in New Brunswick described the action in these words:

"On the 24th inst. Capt. Hyler, of this place, went down with one gun-boat to surprise the Refugee-Town near Sandy-Hook, where the horse thieves resort. He landed within three-quarters of a mile of the light-house, but found that they were out in the country of Monmouth stealing horses. The Captain, however, fell in with six other noted villains, whom he brought off, and they are now lodged in a safe place."

This skirmish failed to sate Hyler's urge for action— and ever more action. Early in November, leaving his whaleboats behind and packing all his men aboard the *Revenge*, he slipped out of the Raritan, veered to the north and coasted along the Staten Island shore until he came to the Narrows. Poking the *Revenge*'s prow inside the channel, he discovered a good-sized cargo ship, the *Father's Desire*, lying in the anchorage close to the Staten Island shore.

Drifting down upon her in the night, Hyler laid the

*Revenge* aboard, and his raiders swept across the bulwarks before the startled British crew of fifteen knew
what was happening. The watch was overpowered and
the crew imprisoned below before the alarm could be
given. Investigating, Hyler found that the *Father's Desire*
had a most desirable cargo of pork and Jamaica rum, and
he decided to take her back to New Brunswick.

Sail was made, and the *Revenge* and *Father's Desire*
stood back through the Narrows, then cut across toward
the New Jersey shore. Again, the trouble was that the
tide was falling, and in trying to cross the shoals between
the Staten Island ship channel and the Raritan River
channel, the *Father's Desire* ran aground off Ward's
Point. Hyler had no choice except to strip and burn her.
He loaded the *Revenge* with all she could carry, some
thirty barrels of pork and twenty hogsheads of rum; took
aboard his fifteen prisoners and a captured Negro slave
named Will; and sailed on up the Raritan, leaving the
*Father's Desire* to burn to the waterline behind him.

This was Hyler's last action of the year. For the rest
of November and all of December, his whaleboat crews
apparently remained inactive, but about the first of the
year, a report reached New Brunswick that sent him off
on a new venture. Patriot spies had learned that a heavily
laden cargo ship was anchored just inside the Narrows.
Hyler decided to try to cut out this rich prize and hastily
assembled the largest flotilla he had yet commanded,
seven whaleboats manned by well over one hundred
men. Leading this squadron in the *Revenge*, he sailed
down the Raritan and made for the Staten Island shore.
On the way he encountered two Tory sloops returning
from a trading voyage to New York. Hyler and his

whaleboatmen promptly gave chase, overhauled the sloops and captured them. It was a rich strike. Both vessels were loaded with dry goods taken in exchange for cargoes delivered in New York, and in addition the whaleboatmen found aboard them some $1,500 in cash.

So much time had been consumed in chasing and capturing the sloops that Hyler had to abandon his projected attack on the heavily laden cargo ship in the Narrows. Instead, he returned to New Brunswick with his prizes, his booty and his prisoners.

Among these was a prominent and notorious Tory, one John "Shore" Stevenson. The capture of Stevenson aroused influential Tories, who began to demand drastic action to wipe out the whaleboat nests along the New Jersey coast. Hyler himself had become such a constant threat that British strategists decided to strike first at his home base of New Brunswick. An attacking force consisting of several hundred veteran British and Tory troops was assembled and ferried across the bay in whaleboats and barges. Shortly after midnight, on the morning of January 7, 1782, the assault force was spotted about two miles from New Brunswick, and the alarm was sounded.

Only a small number of militia was available to oppose the invaders. Townsfolk, thrown into a panic, fled. A few volunteers came forward, and these and the militia tried to prevent the landing. But a driving rain and sleet had dampened many firelocks, and the British and Tories came charging ashore with the loss of only two men killed. The amateur American soldiers, at the sight of the rows of oncoming bayonets, quailed and fled; and the British quickly took possession of the town. They burned the whaleboat fleet and did some looting; then, their mission accomplished, they went back down the river.

In success they had failed: they hadn't been able to find and capture Hyler. Just where he was at the time of the raid isn't clear, but there are some indications that he was cruising in the *Revenge*, for the little sloop seems to have been the only one of his vessels to escape destruction. Returning to New Brunswick, Hyler rushed the construction of new craft for his whaleboaters. He could not replace the destroyed whaleboat fleet, but he built one large barge and a huge thirty-oared whaleboat. With these and the *Revenge*, he was ready for action by the time spring came. It was well that he was.

The British had continued their sweep down the New Jersey coast, landing in raid after raid, burning and destroying salt works, whaleboats and shipyards. These punitive actions led to one final atrocity. In early March, a Tory force stormed the blockhouse at Toms River and captured Captain Joshua Huddy, one of the boldest patriot leaders in Monmouth. Huddy, taken in battle, deserved to be treated with all the honors of war; but the British high command, after holding him a prisoner in New York, turned him over to a Tory leader, Richard Lippincott. Lippincott, a former neighbor of Huddy's, transported his prisoner to a strip of sand at the base of the Navesink highlands, erected a crude gallows, and hanged Huddy out of hand, giving him time only to write his will.

This wanton execution of a brave patriot leader so incensed the Americans that Washington ordered lots drawn for a British officer to be hanged in retaliation. The British were horrified. The prospect of unending tit-for-tat hangings shocked the chancellery in London and made the Huddy affair a matter of international concern.

While diplomats and generals thrashed out the issues, Hyler decided to act. He determined to go right into New York in an attempt to capture Lippincott, the murderer of Huddy.

So daring a scheme required elaborate preparation. Hyler contacted patriot agents on Staten Island and asked them to steal for him the uniforms and accouterments of a Royal Navy press gang. Hyler's Staten Island collaborators pilfered the equipment he needed and even managed to steal a longboat belonging to one of the anchored British warships. Informed that all was ready, Hyler took a picked handful of men and rowed across to Staten Island on a night in early April.

There Hyler donned the uniform, cocked hat and greatcoat of a British lieutenant; his men attired themselves as Royal Navy sailors. Then, with the bogus British tars at the oars, Hyler launched the stolen longboat, took the tiller and, sitting arrogantly erect in the stern, steered his way up the harbor through the thick of the British fleet.

Even after nightfall, British boats were constantly plying these waters on a variety of missions, and so no one paid any attention to the progress of one more press gang. Unchallenged, Hyler and his men completed their long row up the harbor, turned their longboat into the East River and swung boldly in to shore just to the east of the South Ferry landing stages.

Detailing one of his men to guard the boat, Hyler led the rest in a tramping march up Broad Street. On land as in the harbor, the Americans in Royal Navy garb attracted no particular attention. British press gangs were always roving the streets, shanghaiing tipplers from the grog shops to help satisfy the voracious demands of the fleet for ever more manpower. The outcries of impressed victims were a commonplace, so routine that they were usually ignored by passersby, and it was on this that Hyler counted heavily should Lippincott call for help.

It was not yet eleven o'clock when he reached the Lippincott mansion, climbed the steps and hammered authoritatively on the door. He waited, clutching a pistol concealed beneath the folds of his greatcoat.

A Negro servant opened the door, and in a few brief words dealt the death knell to Hyler's bold enterprise. Lippincott wasn't home. He probably wouldn't be home until morning. The British officers were all attending a big party somewhere in town; didn't the lieutenant know?

The "lieutenant" obviously didn't. He excused himself as best he could, telling the Negro he would see his master later. Then he turned and went back down the steps, back to his waiting "press gang." In a few whispered words, Hyler acquainted his men with the mischance that had ruined all their hopes; then he stepped out briskly at their head, retracing the route to the longboat waiting near the ferry stages.

It was not like Hyler to return empty-handed. Foiled in his plan to kidnap Lippincott, he sought some compensation for the hanging he had risked by going into New York in British uniform; and as he headed the longboat out into the stream, he spotted a rum-laden sloop from the West Indies anchored in the fairway.

"Boys," he whispered, gesturing, "we might's well have something to show for our night's trouble. Let's take her."

The boat crew bent to the oars, and in a trice the longboat slid alongside the sloop, whose master was astonished to see a British lieutenant and his press gang swarming up the side at that hour of the night. He was more astonished in the next few minutes, however, by what this strange-acting lieutenant did. The man simply ordered the cable cut, the sails hoisted and the bow headed out into the East River. The man was making off with the whole sloop!

Before the stunned British skipper could make outcry or protest, cutlasses gleamed, and the bogus Royal Navy tars revealed themselves for the Americans they were.

The wind was favoring from the northeast, but Hyler considered the risk of running through the heavily guarded Narrows too great. Therefore, he pointed the sloop's prow farther to the west, ducking into the Kill Van Kull, a narrow thoroughfare that separates the western edge of Staten Island from New Jersey. At Elizabethport, he ran the sloop aground. Wagons were procured, the casks of rum broken out, the sloop stripped. The loot was then hustled away inland, and the sloop, gutted to a shell, was set afire and burned to the water's edge.

The daring attempt to kidnap Lippincott from his own home in the very heart of British-held New York signified that Hyler was again on the warpath; and in the weeks that followed, in a swift succession of actions, each capping the achievements of its predecessor, he left no doubt of it.

The first blow was delivered on a Friday night in late April when Hyler took the *Revenge* and his newly built barge into the Narrows. There he surprised and captured a formidable privateer, a British cutter mounting six eighteen-pounders and ten nine-pounders. Wind and tide being unfavorable, he burned the prize at her mooring. Immediately afterward, he seized a trading sloop, ransomed it back to its owner for $400, and returned to New Brunswick laden with booty and prisoners.

Next, in his big new barge, with twenty-five men, he stole back into the Sandy Hook anchorage where he had made things so hot for the British the previous fall. A heavily armed cutter lay at anchor almost under the guns of the guardship. Fortunately, a thick fog blanketed the bay. Creeping through it, Hyler nudged his barge alongside the cutter, led his men in a pounding charge across the deck and quickly overpowered the sleepy crew. He herded forty prisoners into the barge and the cutter's small boats. Keeping the fastest of the cutter's boats under the counter, he sent his barge and the other boats away into the night. Then he laid a powder train to the cutter's magazine, touched a fuse to it and scrambled over the side. As his waiting men rowed him away into the fog-shrouded night, the cutter blew skyward behind him, showering the bay and the nearby ship-of-the-line with flaming debris.

Just a few days later, near the end of this busy month of April, Hyler took the *Revenge* out to sea on a cruise, and in the Atlantic, barely out of sight of the Sandy Hook lighthouse, he came up on the fast cargo sloop *Alert*, bound from New York to Bermuda with a valuable lading of clothes, shoes, medicines, tea and tools. He snatched the prize and convoyed her into Toms River to be sold.

Riding the crest of success, Hyler now suffered one of those strokes of misfortune that sometimes shadow triumph. The sketchy accounts of the day do not make clear exactly what happened, but Hyler was wounded, the ball from a pistol passing through the flesh of one leg near the knee. The wound was an accidental one—received, one account says, as Hyler picked up a pistol to clean it—and the ball apparently splintered no bones. As events were to show, Hyler was far from incapacitated, but in those days of primitive medicine even trifling wounds could often breed tragic results.

At the time the bullet wound didn't seem even to slow Hyler down. Continuing his cruise down the Jersey coast in the *Revenge,* he encountered the schooner *Speedwell* off Egg Harbor in early May. The *Speedwell,* a taut little craft of twenty-two tons, had belonged to the American firm of Moore & Stratton, but had been captured off the Virginia Capes by the British privateer *Sukey.* She was on her way to New York with a British prize crew aboard. Hyler promptly recaptured her and sent her into Toms River to be sold.

With the seizure of the *Speedwell,* Hyler's luck seemed to run out. He spent some time off the south Jersey coast without a rag of sail showing over the horizon. Provisions started to run low, and he headed the *Revenge* for home. Off Long Branch, he captured a schooner and took her with him through a no-longer-existing inlet called the Gut, which then linked the Shrewsbury River directly with the ocean. Hyler's presence in the Shrewsbury soon became known to Tory spies and, through them, to the British command on Sandy Hook. An expedition was organized to capture the daring privateersman who had tweaked the nose of the Royal Navy with such impunity.

Captain Johann Schaak of the 57th Regiment was

the man selected to snare Hyler. Schaak took a large whaleboat with a swivel mounted in its bow, and with twenty-five regulars rowed down the coast to cut off Hyler's retreat through the Gut. Other forces were to be assembled as quickly as possible and sent down both the bay and ocean sides of the Hook, completing an armed noose from which there would be no escape. But Hyler did not wait for the noose to be drawn.

Learning from his own informants that Schaak had taken up post at the Gut, he determined to surprise the enemy while they were still under the delusion that they were surprising him. He loaded a dozen of his best men into a boat, dropped down the river in the dark and crossed over to Sandy Hook Island (as it was then), landing in Schaak's rear. Advancing stealthily, Hyler crept up on Schaak unobserved and placed his dozen men in ambush around the unsuspecting British camp. As dawn broke, the *Revenge* dropped down the river, stood in close to shore and sprayed the waterside with a deadly hail from her muskets and swivels. While Schaak and his man were preoccupied with this threat from the water, Hyler leaped to his feet in the underbrush and shouted: "Give them a volley, boys, and charge!"

The bushes exploded with musket fire. The heavy balls, fired at close range, tore into the milling figures of the startled regulars. Then the whaleboatmen grabbed their cutlasses and charged the British soldiers with the same impetuosity they used in storming across the decks of unsuspecting merchantmen.

The British, blasted from the inlet by the *Revenge*'s swivels, attacked from the rear by the cutlass-wielding whaleboatmen, threw down their arms and fled. The rout was swift, complete. Hyler, left in possession of the field, captured Captain Schaak and eight of his soldiers. Four others lay dead. The remaining thirteen, some of them badly wounded, escaped into the dunes and underbrush.

Hyler's victory had ensured his escape to sea through the Gut, and he wasted no time. He put his prisoners aboard the *Revenge*, gathered up fifteen stands of arms that the British regulars had left behind them in their flight, and took in tow the swivel-armed whaleboat in which Schaak had come to capture him. Then he stood out to sea, waited for the cover of night and, in the dark, slipped back past the Hook, across the bay and up the Raritan to New Brunswick.

Though that accidental gunshot wound was bothering Hyler, it didn't slow him down. On the last day of June he joined forces with another whaleboat raider, Captain Storer of Woodbridge, and set out on another foray. In the *Revenge*, trailing two whaleboats, he crossed the harbor to Gravesend Bay on the Long Island shore. There he captured two Tory trading sloops and put prize crews aboard. Slipping out to sea past the Hook, he sailed down the coast and brought his prizes through the Gut into the Shrewsbury. He anchored just inside the inlet and sent his two whaleboats up the river. There they captured two more Tory sloops, laden with sheep. When the whaleboats returned, Hyler detached one of them to escort his four prizes down the coast to Toms River. Then, with the rest of his men, he prepared for a new and more ambitious undertaking.

Word had come to him that a fast-sailing privateer, the schooner *Skip Jack*, mounting six large carriage guns and several swivels, was lying at anchor inside the Hook, about two miles from the guardship. She was lightly manned, waiting to take on her full complement before setting out on a cruise. If she could be attacked before her crew was at full strength, she might be carried. Hyler, assessing the chances, determined to make the attempt—at once, in daylight!

For so daring a project, camouflage was obviously needed. Hyler, a man never at a loss for a stratagem, decided to disguise the *Revenge* as a coastal trader. Sending his men ashore, he put them to work cutting lengths of cordwood. These he stacked on the *Revenge*'s deck. His crew would hide behind the piles of wood. The remaining whaleboat was lashed tight against the *Revenge*'s starboard side, where the little sloop's hull would hide it from suspicious eyes as she went up the coast. These preparations completed, Hyler stood out to sea at 10 A.M., July 2, 1782, headed right toward the tip of the Hook.

Rounding the point in full view of the ship-of-the-line, still keeping his whaleboat hidden on the *Revenge*'s off-side, Hyler brought his little sloop about and lazed down toward the anchorage in the cove. Aimlessly, blunderingly, he drifted toward the *Skip Jack*. No clumsy trading sloop could have been handled more ineptly. The sparse crew on the *Skip Jack* suspected nothing until finally, close aboard, Hyler swung into action.

At his shouted order, the cordwood stacked on the *Revenge*'s deck suddenly crawled with men. A full crew tumbled overside into the hidden whaleboat, slashed it loose and pulled for the *Skip Jack*. The *Revenge* in the same instant, waltzing on her heel, swung sharply under the stern of the *Skip Jack*, laying her aboard.

It happened so swiftly that the twelve men on the privateer hardly had time to cry the alarm. Boarders from the whaleboat leaped up the side; Hyler led a second rush across the stern. In the flick of an eye, the *Skip Jack*'s crew were prisoners, their ship taken.

Now Hyler had not a moment to waste. There was not even time to loot. The attack had been made in daylight, in full view of the overwhelmingly superior enemy forces afloat and ashore, and already the decks of the Sandy Hook guardship were stirring with men, milling like a swarm of bees in a ruptured hive.

Hustling his prisoners aboard the *Revenge*, Hyler fired the *Skip Jack* in half a dozen places. Then he cast off and spread the *Revenge*'s white wings in flight. Behind him, flames leaped from deck to rigging aboard the blazing privateer. Behind him, the guns of the log fort ashore barked angrily; the mighty batteries of the guardship thundered in deep-throated and futile menace—just as they had done so many times in the past.

Flames now wreathed the doomed *Skip Jack*, lapped at her carriage guns and exploded them, one by one. Then a spark reached the *Skip Jack*'s magazine, and the world seemed to erupt in one awesome explosion. Flaming rigging and long black spars and huge sections of deck and bulwark were flung skyward, hung suspended for an infinitesimal second, then came raining down in a shower of debris about fort and guardship. It was a thunderous and blazing climax—fittingly so. For this was the last great raid of Adam Hyler.

A couple of lesser expeditions in July marked the finish of his career, for Hyler was now critically ill. Medicine was then a crude science, and the accounts of the day are confused as to the nature of his ailment. One version says he suffered "a tedious and painful illness," resulting from the leg wound he had accidentally inflicted on himself in April. Another account, perhaps inspired by the passions of the times, contended that Hyler had been poisoned by a Tory wench in South Amboy who had slipped a lethal potion into his drink. Though he was not killed instantly, the effects were such that he never recovered.

Whatever the cause, Hyler was doomed. He died at his home in New Brunswick on September 6, 1782, and was buried in the old Dutch burial ground. Ten days later his wife, Ann, gave birth to a son—a boy named Adam, who was to grow up to become a skipper and to sail his own ships across the waters of New York harbor on which his father had fought.

# VII
★★★★★★★
# Silas Talbot

IT WAS characteristic of the men of the Revolution that they were a many-sided breed, as much at home on the sea as on land. They could fight with equal skill in either element, and it was not unusual for the army captain to become a sea captain. Benedict Arnold, before he turned traitor, commanded ships as well as regiments and fought as furiously on Lake Champlain as he did later on the field of Saratoga. Among the privateersmen, none filled this dual role more brilliantly than Major-Captain Silas Talbot of Rhode Island.

Talbot was born of poor parents in Dighton, Massachusetts, and went to sea as a cabin boy on a coastal trader when he was only twelve. By the time he was twenty-one, he was the master of his own vessel and had saved enough money to build himself a house in Providence, Rhode Island.

When the Revolution broke out, he was commissioned a captain in a Rhode Island regiment that took

151

part in the siege of Boston. After the British evacuated that port, Talbot's regiment was transferred to New York, arriving after the city had already fallen to the British. Washington and his disorganized army had begun the long retreat to the north up the Hudson River, and the Royal Navy sent warships upstream to try to cut off the American flight to New Jersey.

Washington had no warships with which to oppose the enemy and so decided on a gamble—to attack the British with fire ships. Talbot volunteered for this hazardous mission, and he and Ensign Thomas were given command of two river sloops crammed with combustibles. Three British warships, headed by the sixty-four-gun ship-of-the-line *Asia*, lay at anchor seven miles upriver from New York, and Talbot was ordered to attack them.

Picking a night when wind and tide were favorable, he weighed anchor about two o'clock in the morning and dropped downriver toward the British warships. The target he selected for himself was the most powerful of the three—the *Asia*. As his little sloop slid quietly through the water, Talbot had his men drench her flammable cargo with turpentine and lay fresh powder trains. He sent a man named Priestly, an excellent swimmer, to the forecastle with a lighted match to make certain that the powder trains fore and aft were ignited at the same instant.

The fire ship ghosted silently through the night, Talbot hoping to catch the British by surprise, but the *Asia*'s watch was alert. An alarm was shouted as Talbot's sloop drew near, and guns began to fire. Several shots passed through the hull of Talbot's little craft, but failed to sink or stop her. She came jarring alongside the

*Asia*, and Priestly and Talbot touched lighted matches to their powder trains.

Talbot had sent the rest of his crew away in the ship's boat just before the impact, and it was well that he had. Flames burst forth in one wild conflagration almost the instant the powder trains were ignited. The whole hull of the little fire ship was wreathed in flames, and Talbot and Priestly were almost trapped. Priestly escaped by plunging from the forecastle into the river, where he was picked up by the ship's boat, but Talbot had to dash through a wall of fire before he could reach a sally port and leap.

He was rescued by his boat crew in a sorry condition. The clothes had been burned off his back; his face and hands were scorched; and the fierce heat of the fire had singed his eyebrows and eyelashes and left him for the moment unable to see.

His men pulled frantically away from the raging inferno in the river, where the flames from the fire ship were leaping up the sides of the *Asia*. The white heat of the blaze lighted up the dark waters for miles around, and the little boat stood out as if painted on canvas, an inviting target. Guns from the British warships thundered, and their iron balls lashed the water all around the fleeing boat. Fortunately, in the surprise and confusion, the aim was hurried and bad, and Talbot's men pulled out of range unscathed.

Behind them, the crew of the *Asia*, aided by sailors from the other ships, worked at frantic speed to extinguish the fires that threatened the huge ship-of-the-line. In this they succeeded. The *Asia* was scorched, but the damage was minor.

The fire ship raid had failed to accomplish its

purpose, but it had not been entirely futile. The narrow escape of the *Asia* alarmed the captains of the warships. Not knowing when they might be attacked again, they ordered their ships' cables slipped and dropped hurriedly down the river, anchoring in safety in the harbor off the lower part of Manhattan. The way had been opened for Washington's retreat across the Hudson into New Jersey.

Talbot and his men escaped to the New Jersey shore. The captain was so burned and blistered that his eyes were swollen shut and he could not see. His men led him, blind and suffering, through the woods, seeking help. They were turned away at several houses because Talbot's appearance was so horrible he frightened the homeowners and their children. Finally, a poor widow living in a small log hut took him in, and he was stretched out on the floor and covered with a blanket.

Fortunately, General Henry Knox, in charge of Washington's artillery, heard about his plight and brought an army surgeon to treat him. Talbot, a stocky man with a rugged constitution, slowly battled his way back to health. Congress, in recognition of his daring, promoted him to major.

Ensign Thomas, who had commanded the other fire ship, was not so fortunate. He brought his vessel alongside a fourteen-gun British tender in Tappan Bay, set fire to her and destroyed her. But Thomas, unlike Talbot, did not escape in time; he perished in the flames he had ignited.

After Talbot had recovered, he rejoined his regiment, which was assigned to defend Fort Mifflin on the lower Delaware. In November, 1777, the British, who had captured Philadelphia, then the capital of the rebelling colonies, sent their fleet and army units to reduce the American forts on the river and clear the channel for passage of their supply ships.

The American defenders, though hopelessly outnumbered, put up a spirited defense. A musket ball shattered Talbot's left wrist, but the new major simply wrapped a handkerchief around the wound and kept on fighting. Shortly afterward, he was struck down by another ball that penetrated his hip and disabled him. With other wounded he was rowed to the New Jersey shore at Red Bank, then sent to a hospital in Princeton. Partially recovered, he received Washington's permission to return to his home in Providence, Rhode Island, for his wounds to heal.

This transfer to Providence resulted in a whole new career for Talbot, one that gradually transformed him from an army major into a privateering captain.

The British had overrun the lower part of Rhode Island, seizing Newport at the southern tip and closing the river channels leading to Providence. In the campaign of 1778, a French fleet under Count d'Estaing was scheduled to cooperate with American land forces in an attempt to take Newport. In order to ferry American troops across the river channels for the attack, large barges had to be built, and Talbot was put in charge of their construction. He drove his workmen so hard that sixteen barges were finished in a single day, the final calking of their bottoms being done by candlelight.

Eighty-six boats were completed by August 9, when the embarkation of American troops began. Talbot went with the forces that were ferried across to the island of Rhode Island for the march south against Newport. Reconnoitering in advance of his troops, he came within sight of the British fort and spotted three enemy artillery-men outside the lines, foraging in a garden.

Leaping his horse over a wall, Talbot drew his sword and charged down upon the three soldiers, threatening to kill them instantly. They apparently mistook him at first for one of their own officers and begged him not to report them for punishment. Talbot, promising nothing, took their arms from them, then marched them before him back to the American lines.

The campaign against Newport was a total failure. The French fleet failed to cooperate, and the Americans were forced to retreat to the mainland. One side effect of the campaign, however, had been the temporary opening of the river channels. When the French fleet first appeared, the British had scuttled some of their warships, including the frigate *Flora*. With the departure of the French, the British command in Newport determined to block the passages to American commerce once more.

They converted a stout brig of some two hundred tons into a galley by removing her upper deck. Eight twelve-pounders from the *Flora* were mounted on her, and ten swivels were fastened to her bulwarks. Manned by a crew of forty-five men, protected by strong boarding nettings, this craft was named the *Pigot* in honor of the commanding British general, Sir Robert Pigot; and she was stationed in the eastern passage, completely closing that important channel to vessels bound for Providence.

The Americans needed to rid themselves of the *Pigot* for the sake of their all-important sea-borne traffic. And so in early October Talbot obtained permission from his army superiors to fit out a privateer. He obtained a small seventy-ton coasting schooner named the *Hawk*, mounted two puny three-pounders on her, and manned her with a crew of sixty men who answered his call for volunteers.

The *Pigot* was anchored off Black Point in the Sakonnet River on the east side of Rhode Island. To get at her, Talbot had to run past two British forts. The first was located at the northern tip of the island, its guns covering the Bristol Ferry channel, there only three-quarters of a mile wide.

Choosing a night when he had a favorable breeze, Talbot took the *Hawk* through the Bristol Ferry channel, hugging the opposite shore from the British fort. He was discovered and fired on, but in the night the enemy's aim was bad, and the *Hawk* got past the battery untouched. Talbot then veered to the north, running about six miles up the Taunton River and anchoring on the west side of Mount Hope Bay. He was now about fifteen miles north of the *Pigot*, and he still had to run past the second British battery at Fogland Ferry on the Sakonnet River.

Since he had to wait for a shift of wind to make his final run, he decided to reconnoiter the *Pigot* personally. He landed on the east side of the Sakonnet, obtained a horse and rode down the shore until he reached a point opposite the galley. Undetected, he studied the *Pigot* through his telescope at leisure.

She was, he decided, a much more formidable foe than he had been led to believe. Her boarding nettings were carried very high and were wrapped around the entire vessel, so that it would be extremely difficult to hack a way through them and carry her by boarding. Yet boarding represented the only opportunity the Americans had, for the *Pigot*'s menacing twelve-pounders could blow the *Hawk* out of the water, given a chance.

Mulling over the difficulty, Major Talbot rode back

up the shore and rejoined his crew. He decided that he needed more help and obtained an additional army detail of fifteen men under Lieutenant Helm, of Rhode Island. When these reinforcements reached the *Hawk*, Talbot called all hands aft and made a rousing speech. He offered a reward for the first man who reached the galley's deck, and he promised to capture the *Pigot* if his men kept cool and did their duty. The men cheered.

That same night, the wind favoring, Talbot got the *Hawk* under way at nine o'clock. He lashed a large kedge anchor to his little schooner's jib boom in the hope that, if he succeeded in running alongside the *Pigot*, the anchor would tear a gap in those high boarding nettings through which his men could charge.

The Fogland Ferry battery worried him, and so, approaching it, he ordered all sails stripped off the *Hawk*. Under bare poles, carried by the tide, she drifted quietly past, so close to the battery that sentinels could be seen silhouetted against the night every time they strolled past a beam of light coming from the barracks windows. Fortunately, none of them spotted the *Hawk* as she glided into the lower river, set her sails and headed for the *Pigot* just four miles away.

Not finding the galley as soon as he had anticipated, Talbot began to wonder if he had overshot his mark and ordered the *Hawk* anchored. Then he took a small boat and, with muffled oars, slipped quietly off into the night. He soon found the galley lying directly ahead of him, crept up close to her and fixed in his mind a clear picture of just how she lay in the tide and wind.

Then, returning to the *Hawk*, he ordered sail hoisted once more and headed for the *Pigot*. The British watch spotted the approaching schooner and hailed. Talbot gave no answer, but bore steadily down upon the foe. Repeated hails went unanswered, and the British, now thoroughly aroused, fired their muskets at the approaching *Hawk*. There was no time for more, no time to run out and fire the great guns, for the *Hawk* came crashing and slithering alongside, her kedge anchor tearing a great gap in those protective boarding nettings.

"Boarders away!" shouted Talbot.

Lieutenant Helm and his army contingent, wielding long pikes, led the charge and gained the galley's deck. The surprised British crew quickly abandoned the fight and fled below. Their commander, Lieutenant Dunlop, appeared on deck in his underwear and tried to rally his men, but he was soon overpowered and forced to surrender.

When he learned that his formidable galley had been captured by a tiny coaster mounting only two three-pounders, the young lieutenant burst into tears. He had, he said, "fancied himself to stand as fair a chance for promotion as any lieutenant in the navy," but now he saw himself disgraced, all hope for advancement destroyed.

A check showed that not a man on either side had been killed in the brief fray. The prisoners were sent below and securely penned in by coiling heavy cables over the gratings, weighting them down so that they could not be forced. Then Talbot got both vessels under way and ran down the coast to Stonington, Connecticut, where the prisoners were landed and marched overland to Providence.

This exploit greatly raised "the spirit of the people," according to a contemporary account. Congress rewarded Talbot with promotion to lieutenant colonel, and

the General Assembly of Rhode Island presented com-
memorative swords to both Talbot and Helm.

The new army colonel now devoted his talents
exclusively to the sea. Though his capture of the *Pigot*
had opened the Rhode Island coast to commerce, the
Americans found themselves unable to take advantage of
the opportunity. Tory privateers, fitted out in New York,
were sweeping Long Island Sound and the Connecticut
and Rhode Island coasts, preying on American shipping
to such an extent that few captains dared venture out of
port. General Gates, in command of the northern depart-
ment, reported to Washington that it was almost impossible to secure provisions for the army, because coast-
wise commerce was at a standstill.

To remedy the situation, the army took possession
of a one-hundred-ton sloop whose owner was absent in
New York. She was named the *Argo*, and a less warlike-
looking warship never existed. She was fitted out with an
armament of twelve six-pounders, but she was no seagoing gazelle. She had very high bulwarks and a wide,
waddling stern like that of "a clumsy Albany sloop."
Instead of the conventional wheel, she was steered by a
long tiller.

Talbot got together a crew of sixty volunteers from
the army, most of whom had been seamen, and sailed
from Providence on his first cruise in May, 1779. He
rounded the eastern end of Long Island and there sighted
the Tory privateer *Lively*, mounting like the *Argo* twelve
six-pounders. Though the ships were of equal strength,
the *Lively* showed no eagerness to fight, and Talbot
chased her for five hours before he got alongside. Then
the *Lively*, showing no liveliness, tamely surrendered.

Talbot sent her into port with a prize crew and

continued his cruise. Some three days later, he encountered two English privateers bound from the West Indies to New York and heavily laden. He compelled both to surrender without much of a struggle, put prize crews aboard them and sent them into Boston.

Such swift, tame victories were only preludes to more exciting action to come. One Tory privateer, the stout brig *King George*, mounting fourteen six-pounders and manned by a crew of eighty men, had especially infuriated Rhode Islanders. This craft had been fitted out in Newport and was commanded by Captain Stanton Hazard, a native Rhode Islander of good reputation "till he took command of this privateer for the base purpose of plundering his neighbors and old friends."

Hazard had plundered with such success that he had become a much-hated man. Whenever Talbot put into a port along the Sound for the night, as he sometimes did, he heard denunciations of Hazard and the *King George*. Though the *King George* was a more powerful craft than the *Argo*, Talbot was anxious to hunt down this detested Tory raider.

On his second cruise, some 120 miles at sea south of Long Island, a sail was sighted in the distance on an extremely clear, calm and beautiful day. The stranger was obviously a warship, for she made no attempt to run. Forging steadily through the gently rolling seas, the two vessels approached each other, and when they were close, Talbot hailed. Captain Hazard in person answered him, and the battle was joined.

The *Argo* fired her broadside into the *King George*, then bored through the powder smoke to crash alongside. Once more Talbot called for boarders, and his men swept over the *Argo*'s high bulwarks and down upon the deck of the Tory privateer. So sudden was the onslaught that the fight on the enemy deck was over almost before it had begun. The Tory crew fled below and were imprisoned. Not a man on either side had been killed.

Talbot put a prize crew aboard the *King George* and sent her into New London, where cheering crowds, including women and children, gathered at the waterfront to stare at the Tory privateer that had done so much damage—and, in the end, had yielded so tamely.

The bloodless victories continued. Talbot came across an American privateer that had been captured by the British, retook her and sent her into New Bedford, Massachusetts. Shortly afterward, he encountered the merchant brig *Elliott*, bound from London for New York with a valuable cargo of dry goods and provisions. She was taken without a struggle and sent into New London.

The *Argo*, unlikely craft, had now taken six prizes without the loss of a man. In the nature of things, such luck could not be expected to continue forever. Nor did it.

Early on an August morning, Talbot in his "army privateer" discovered a large ship standing toward him. As she came closer, it could easily be seen that she was a warship, large, well-armed and full of men. Talbot saw that she was a much larger and more powerful vessel than the *Argo*, but he held to his course and came up within pistol shot of the stranger. Hails were exchanged, defiances uttered—and the battle began.

Broadside to broadside, so close at times that the hulls almost touched, the two ships pounded at each other. For four and a half hours the battle raged, the great guns thundering, muskets and pistols spitting fire. The speaking trumpet that Talbot held to his mouth was pierced by shot in two places, and a cannon ball sheared off the tail of his coat. Still the battle raged on.

The *Argo*'s fire was so well-directed that nearly all the men stationed on the enemy's quarter deck were killed or wounded. Finally, her mainmast, splintered by roundshot, gave way with a large cracking sound and slowly toppled into the sea. Helpless, unable to maneuver with this tangled mass of rigging over the side, the British finally surrendered. Their privateer was the *Dragon*, a ship of 300 tons, mounting fourteen six-pounders and manned by a crew of eighty men.

Talbot had no time to exult over this conquest of an opponent three times the *Argo*'s size, for even as the *Dragon*'s mainmast was toppling, the *Argo* began to sink. One of Talbot's officers, stationed at the magazine below deck, sent word that water was pouring in and reaching almost to the level of the gun deck. A hasty examination showed that the *Argo* had been so riddled by the *Dragon*'s roundshot she was taking in water through several holes smashed in her hull near the waterline.

Sailors were swung over the side to plug these shot holes, and others of the crew manned the pumps to clear the foundering sloop of water. Gradually, the sea's inrush slowed as hole after hole was plugged, and strenuous work at the pumps cleared the *Argo*'s hold.

A prize crew was put aboard the *Dragon*, a jury mast rigged, and she was sent off to New Bedford. She was still in sight, limping away, when another sail loomed above the horizon. This turned out to be the English privateer brig *Hannah*, of 200 tons, carrying twelve twelve-pounders and two six-pounders, an armament capable of throwing more than double the *Argo*'s weight of broadside metal.

Undaunted, Talbot waded in and tackled the *Hannah* in another fierce broadside duel. Fortunately, shortly after this second battle began, yet another sail hove into sight. This turned out to be the Pennsylvania privateer *Macaroni*, mounting only six guns. She came on and joined in the fray, her popguns blazing; and the *Hannah*, though of superior force to both her antagonists combined, became discouraged at the two-to-one odds and surrendered.

These two fierce actions in one day and the riddled condition of his ship made Talbot decide to head for New Bedford with the *Dragon* and the *Hannah*. The arrival of the three ships created a local sensation. A contemporary account gives this description:

"When the *Argo* returned to port with these last prizes she was so shivered in her hull and rigging by the shot which had pierced her in the last two engagements that all who beheld her were astonished that a vessel of her diminutive size could suffer so much and yet get safely into port. The country people came down from a considerable distance, only to see Captain Talbot and his prizes and to count the shot marks about the *Argo*."

Talbot's succession of victories with such a puny privateer so impressed Congress that he was commissioned a captain in the navy. He was now in the strange position of being both a navy captain and an army lieutenant colonel; but, since there was no ship available for him to command, he continued to draw his Army pay. And as soon as the battered *Argo* could be repaired, he went back to sea.

He set a course for Sandy Hook and there joined forces with Captain Munroe, commanding the Providence privateer *Saratoga*. On a clear moonlight night, they spotted the Tory privateer *Dublin* coming out of the harbor. The two captains decided to use the tiny *Argo* as bait to lure the *Dublin* away from shore and into battle. Carrying out this strategy, Talbot took his little privateer in close, while Munroe remained almost out of sight in the offing.

The *Dublin* bit, anticipating an easy victory. Too late, she discovered she had caught a Tartar. The *Argo* battled the stronger Tory craft broadside to broadside for two hours; then the *Saratoga*, which had been delayed by tiller trouble, came up and poured in her broadside, ending the battle.

The two American privateers, having pulled off this daring coup almost under the noses of the British and Tories on Sandy Hook, made off quickly down the coast with their prize. On the way the *Argo* seized the 200-ton British brig *Chance*, laden with a valuable cargo of stores for the British Army. Then Talbot and Munroe took their two prizes into Egg Harbor to be sold.

Talbot scored one more major victory in the little *Argo*. On his way back to Providence, he encountered a large British privateer, the *Betsey*, a brig pierced for sixteen guns but mounting just twelve six-pounders. After a spirited hour-long battle that left all her officers either killed or wounded, the *Betsey* hauled down her colors, and Talbot took her into port with him.

On landing, Talbot found orders instructing him to give the *Argo* back to her rightful owner, Nicholas Law of New York, from whom she had been appropriated without so much as a by-your-leave. This ended the phenomenally successful career of the tiny "army privateer." For such a small and clumsy craft, never intended for warfare, the achievements of the *Argo* and her commander touched on the incredible. She had sent into port more than a dozen prizes of great value. She had taken some three hundred prisoners, bodies that were valuable in arranging exchanges for captured Americans. She had virtually cleared Long Island Sound and the adjacent coasts of marauding Tory privateers. And so she had opened the sea lanes for the transport of supplies so badly needed by the northern army. Quite a record for a clumsy-looking 100-ton "Albany sloop."

Talbot's career, with its string of uninterrupted victories, now did a sudden about-face. In the summer of 1780 he was given command of a newly built Providence privateer—a vessel so swift, tall-masted and well-armed that she made the poor *Argo* look like a ferryboat. His new command was the *General Washington*, a powerful vessel mounting twenty six-pounders and carrying a crew of 120 men.

At first, Talbot's luck seemed to hold. Soon after putting to sea, he captured a valuable merchantman bound from Charleston, South Carolina, to London, and sent her into Boston. Then he took a British ship bound from the West Indies to Ireland, but this prize was recaptured before she could reach port.

Talbot next headed for the rewarding but dangerous hunting ground off Sandy Hook, where he had lured the *Dublin* into battle. And it was here that his luck gave out. He ran into the heart of a British fleet.

The *General Washington* was an extremely fast vessel, but weather conditions were against her. The wind was blowing a gale; and in such a wind a ship-of-the-line, massive of hull and heavily sparred, could carry a greater press of sail than smaller craft. This is what happened now. The huge *Culloden*, flaunting a cloud of canvas that would have capsized the *General Washington* or torn the masts out of her, ran the privateer down and forced her to surrender.

Talbot was brutally treated and sent to prison in England. He was exchanged in October, 1781; sailed for home aboard a Rhode Island brig; and was captured again by a British privateer when only fifteen days at sea. His new captor treated him with far greater kindness than had the gentlemen of the Royal Navy. He decided that Talbot had suffered enough and put him aboard a British brig bound for New York. Arriving in that enemy stronghold, Talbot skipped quickly across to Long Island, hid out for a week, then crossed the Sound to the Connecticut shore in a small boat on a dark night. And so, eventually, he made his way home.

In the postwar era, Talbot's dual army colonel–navy captain role came to an end. He stuck with the navy and became one of the first commanders of the most famous frigate in American naval history—the never-defeated *Constitution*.

# VIII
★★★★★★★

# The Accomplishments

THE AMERICAN privateers that swarmed by the thousands from our own coastal waters to the West Indies and the shores of Great Britain played an important role—one that has been too little recognized—in the winning of the Revolution.

In the latter part of the war, American shipbuilders began to exercise their ingenuity by designing and launching a new class of large, fast-sailing vessels built expressly for privateering. Such private warships, some as heavily armed as small frigates, represented enormous advances in speed, maneuverability and power over the lumbering converted merchantmen and hastily armed fishing smacks that had put to sea to prey on British commerce in the early years.

Typical of the new type of warships were the lofty *Grand Turk* of Salem and the lightning-fast brig *Holker* of Philadelphia. The *Grand Turk* was built for Elias Hasket Derby, the famous Salem shipowner. She was a full-rigged ship of 300 tons, carried a frigate's armament of twenty-eight guns, and was manned by a crew of 120 men.

The *Grand Turk* put to sea on her maiden cruise in the latter part of June, 1781, and from that time until the end of the war she was ceaselessly on the prowl, ranging the seas from the American coast to the British Isles and the West Indies. So awesome was her armament that she fought no pitched battles, the vessels she overhauled yielding to the menace of her overwhelming row of gunports.

Except for her first cruise, the *Grand Turk* was under the command of Captain Thomas Pratt, a stocky, round-faced Salem shipmaster, grim of features, with hard eyes deep-set under heavy brows, and a wide strong mouth that bit down at the corners like the flanges of a steel trap. Under Pratt, the *Grand Turk* sailed directly for the Irish coast in late October, 1781; and there, in plain sight of Queenstown, she captured a remarkably rich prize, the large ship *Mary* loaded with "upwards of 900 Hogsheads of Sugar some Coffee & Kampecehe wood." The *Mary* had been so close to shore when taken that Pratt let her crew take some of her boats and row to land before he made off with his prize to Bilbao, Spain.

Several of the *Grand Turk*'s prizes were worth more individually than it had cost Derby to build his frigate-like privateer, and the total returns from her enterprise were enormous. In the last year and ten months of the war, the *Grand Turk* captured sixteen British vessels and was lucky enough to get all her prizes into port to be sold. Her last capture, and one of the best, was the 400-ton twenty-gun ship *Pompey*, taken in the West Indies in early March, 1783, after the treaty of peace had been signed in Paris but before word of it had reached America. The *Pompey*, sent into Salem, was sold to another prominent Salem shipowner, George Crowninshield. Renamed the *America*, she became the first of three famous vessels of that name to carry the Crowninshield house flag in international trade.

The *Holker*, built more to sloop-of-war dimensions, had a longer career than the *Grand Turk* and became so famous she was dubbed "the mischievous *Holker*" by the British and "the millionaire maker" by the Americans. She was an extremely fast sixteen-gun brig built especially for privateering by Blair McClenahan of Philadelphia. She got to sea in April, 1779.

She was commanded at first by George Geddes; and in two privateering cruises under Geddes, she took so many prizes that she made her skipper so wealthy he retired from the sea. Her first cruise netted six rich prizes, one a large ship loaded with eighty cannon for the British Army. The proceeds of this cruise alone were reported to have amounted to an incredible one million British pounds. Geddes's own profits from his two cruises in the *Holker* were estimated at 100,000 pounds, a veritable fortune in those days. No wonder he could retire!

Matthew Lawler commanded the *Holker* on her third cruise, and he was so successful he needed only this one foray, instead of Geddes's two, to quit the sea and enjoy the comforts of land. Captain Roger Keane succeeded Lawler and handled the *Holker* on her fourth cruise, during which she took so many prizes it was estimated that her owner cleared one million pounds on this voyage alone.

The *Holker* by this time had become such a menace

to British shipping that several warships were sent out for the express purpose of hunting her down. She had several narrow escapes but sailed so fast she showed her heels to all her pursuers. It seemed too much to expect such good fortune to last forever, and so the word that reached Philadelphia in April, 1781, was widely credited. Rumor had it the *Holker* had been captured. But rumor, as in so many cases, was soon proved wrong. On June 3 the *Holker* was sighted off the Delaware Capes, standing in to port. She had just completed one of her more remunerative cruises. She had taken fourteen prizes in the West Indies and had made Captain Keane such a wealthy man that he too now quit the sea and retired.

Captain John Quinlan succeeded Keane, and the *Holker* lined his pockets just as she had done those of his predecessors. In one six-week period, she took sixteen British vessels. But then, on March 2, 1783—ironically, after peace had already been declared in Europe—her luck ran out. The *Holker*, back on her favorite West Indies cruising grounds, was pursued by a British frigate. She cracked on all sail to escape and seemed to be showing the frigate her usual clean pair of heels when a sudden squall howled down upon both vessels. When it passed, the frigate was alone on the sea. The *Holker*, carrying too much sail, had been unable to strip her yards in time; she had capsized and sunk. Boats from the frigate were lowered and picked up forty-seven survivors out of her complement of more than one hundred.

Such were the exploits of American privateersmen. From the days when the little *Lee* supplied Washington with the weapons he needed for his army to the very end of the war, the privateers took a heavy toll of British commerce, raised hob with insurance rates, supplied

America with much-needed arms and equipment, and intensified internal pressures on the British government to conclude a peace.

Estimates of the value of the prizes taken by the privateers range all over the landscape, from a low of $18 million to a high of nearly $66 million. The latter figure, which includes seizures by the Continental Navy, is based on the records of one of the most reliable barometers, Lloyd's of London. These showed that 3,087 British merchant ships were taken during the war, with 879 ransomed or retaken. This left some 2,208 vessels that were either destroyed at sea or reached port safely to be sold as prizes. In addition, Lloyd's figures showed that the Americans had taken eighty-nine British privateers, of which only fourteen had been recaptured.

Since the Continental Navy was almost nonexistent during the whole last three years of the war, privateers accounted for the bulk of these losses. The privateers and the Navy together took some 16,000 British seamen prisoners during the war—a figure that compares favorably with the 22,000 Redcoats captured by the American Army in all its battles.

The effects of privateering on the new nation were profound and continued to be felt long after the war itself had ended. Privateering had placed enormous wealth— resources far beyond the dreams of most Americans in colonial times—in the hands of a new class of shipping and merchant princes. A Salem chronicler of the day reflected: "Those who five years ago were the meaner people are now, by a strange revolution, become almost the only men of power, riches, and influence. The Cabots, of Beverly, who, you know, had but five years ago a very moderate share of property, are now said to be the most wealthy in New England; Hasket Derby claims second place on the list."

This new affluence gave birth to an era of maritime expansion. The 100-ton sloops and schooners, sufficient for coastal trading and short voyages to the West Indies, were supplanted by large, well-found vessels ranging the distant seas. Some, like the *Pompey* that became the *America*, were majestic ships that had been captured from the British; others like the *Grand Turk*, a private frigate turned merchantman, had been financed by successful privateering ventures. Such ships were soon carrying the American flag around Cape Horn to the Pacific Northwest and around the Cape of Good Hope to tap the wealth of the East Indies.

The privateers of seventy-six, a heroic breed, had not merely helped to win a war, an achievement enough in itself; they had given birth to a whole new era that saw the American flag carried to the remotest corners of the world.